United States Olympic Comm

Curriculum Guide to the Olympic Games

36 USC 220506

Volume II

Share the Olympic Dream

INTERMEDIATE

Griffin Publishing Group
Torrance, California

Share the Olympic Dream

10 9 8 7 6

ISBN 1-58000-057-6

Griffin Publishing Group and Teacher Created Materials, Inc. wish to thank the many talented and devoted supporters of the Olympic Games who made this publication possible.

DIRECTOR of OPERATIONS	Robin Howland	EDITOR	Evan D. Forbes, M.S. Ed.
PROJECT MANAGER	Bryan Howland	WRITER	Cynthia Holzschuher
COVER DESIGN	Chris Macabitas	ILLUSTRATOR	Phil Hopkins

U.S. OLYMPIC COMMITTEE

William J. Hybl	President
Richard D. Schultz	Executive Director
Dave Ogrean	Deputy Executive Director, Marketing
Mike Moran	Assistant Executive Director, Media and Public Affairs
Barry King	Director, Marketing/Fund Raising Communications
Sheila Walker	Senior Director, Sport Development
Velinda Baker	Director, Education Resources

Griffin Publishing Group
2908 Oregon Court, Suite 1-5
Torrance, CA 90503

Published in association with and distributed by

Teacher Created Materials, Inc.
6421 Industry Way
Westminister, CA 92683
www.teachercreated.com

Manufactured in the USA

Table of Contents

Table of Contents (cont.)

Introduction

Every two years there is a special excitement in the air. The eyes and ears of the world are on athletes who meet in friendly competition to see who is the fastest runner, the highest jumper, the speediest skier, the most graceful skater. It is the continuation of a tradition begun long ago in the Valley of Olympia in ancient Greece—the Olympic Games. Top athletes from around the world compete for medals signifying that they are the best. This book is about the Olympic Games competition. The official designation, Olympic Games, refers to the Games held during the summer months every four years. The Games held in the winter months every four years are officially know as the Olympic Winter Games. Included in this book are ideas, materials, and activities that can be used with students in the intermediate and middle-school grades.

The contents are designed to provide the following:

- Information and practice activities to familiarize students with the Olympic Games
- Creative worksheets to challenge students to recall and apply what they have learned
- A complete game to bring the spirit of the Olympic Games to your classroom
- Plans for an academic pentathlon and mini-Olympic Games
- Suggestions for additional activities and enrichment
- A teacher resource package including bulletin board and research center ideas, art patterns, an answer key, and bibliography

The materials presented are adaptable for:

- Class or group lessons
- Independent research
- Cooperative learning activities

The Olympic Games, usually held in July or August when many students are on vacation, may be introduced to them at the end of the traditional school year. Thus, they can better appreciate the Games on television or in person.

The Olympic Winter Games, held in January or February when most schools are in session, offer the opportunity for additional activities based on the daily schedule of the Games.

The hope for peace is renewed at the Olympic Games. When the Olympic flag is flying and the Olympic flame is burning, we think of world peace and cooperation. As we watch the ceremonies and competitions, we appreciate and respect the talents of individual athletes. Differences in nationalities fade as similarities in human spirit emerge.

This is the spirit of the Olympic Games. We hope this book will bring this spirit alive for you and your students.

Planning Your Olympic Games Experience

Although the Olympic Games may not be familiar to all of your students, this publication will make it easy for you to develop knowledgeable, well-informed sports enthusiasts. This will be especially true if the Games are in progress as you teach this material.

Begin to organize your source materials a few weeks in advance. Most useful will be encyclopedias, current almanacs, sports encyclopedias and almanacs, publications of the U.S. Olympic Games Committee, and books of the Official U.S. Olympic Games Committee Sports Series from Griffin Publishing. In addition, the bibliography in this book cites several resources, and your local library will offer other selections.

Create an exciting bulletin board display. Here is an idea that will motivate your students by involving them in its construction. When you tell them they will be starting a unit on the Olympic Games, it will be easy to elicit the names of some popular events. Reproduce and cut apart the logos of the Olympic Games events (pages 128–134). Give one to each student along with a six-inch (15 cm) square of black construction paper. Students are to enlarge the logos. (It helps to use a penny to make all the "heads" the same size.) Then pass another six-inch (15 cm) square of construction paper to each student. (Vary the colors: red, blue, green, yellow.) The students glue their own logos on the colored squares. Arrange them on the bulletin board as shown below. Students who finish early may help to construct a large Olympic Games flag to be placed in the middle of the display. (The ring pattern is on page 124.)

Planning Your Olympic Games Experience (cont.)

Plan how you wish to teach this unit.

Class Lessons

You may intend to teach the Olympic Games as one of your social studies units, devoting a regular period to it each day. In that case, you will probably want to use this book page by page while working with your class. Do not forget to use the additional activities (page 116), as well as your own creativity.

Center Approach

You may wish to combine a research center with your class lessons. However, the lessons in this book may also be used as a separate, independent center. If you are using the Olympic Games as an enrichment to your regular program, this would be appropriate.

To set up your center, use the bulletin board as a background or choose another appropriate area.

You may wish to construct the center with three sheets of poster board. Trim large manila envelopes and attach them to the side panels. Reproduce and place appropriate pages and forms in these pockets. The center panel can be decorated with the Olympic Games rings and a paper placed below detailing your expectations. Place all necessary supplies at the center—construction paper, scissors, glue, etc. Make the directions short and clear. Example:

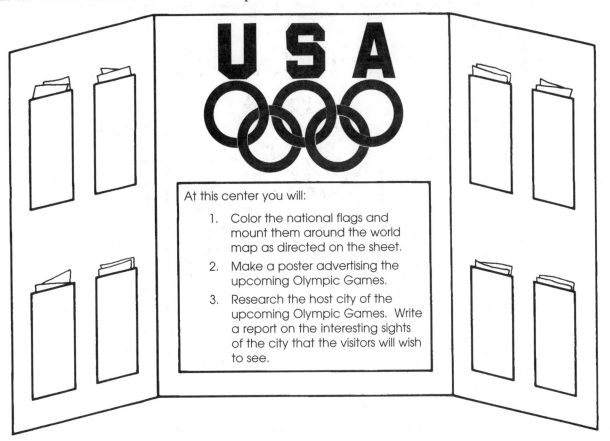

At this center you will:

1. Color the national flags and mount them around the world map as directed on the sheet.
2. Make a poster advertising the upcoming Olympic Games.
3. Research the host city of the upcoming Olympic Games. Write a report on the interesting sights of the city that the visitors will wish to see.

Planning Your Olympic Games Experience (cont.)

A study center can be an effective venue for teaching and individualizing instruction. How you arrange and develop the study center ultimately influences its overall effectiveness. Let your own creativity, combined with your perceptions of your students' abilities, be your guide.

Introduce the center by explaining what it is and how it is to be used, and convey your expectations in detail. Make your students aware of what they should accomplish (both collectively and individually), and give them completion dates for each assignment. Completed work may be collected and kept at the study center, or students can make folders and keep their projects at their desks.

Class Lesson/ Center Approach

1. Set up your center for one unit at a time.

   As you conduct your group lessons, students may use the center for one or more research projects related to that unit. Here are some suggested activities appropriate for center use:

   - Olympic Games History—Report on Greek gods related to the Olympic Games: Zeus, Hera, Demeter; or on famous Olympians: Milo of Croton, Leonidas of Rhodes, etc.
   - Make a poster advertising the Games.
   - Design medals (page 121).
   - Olympic Games Traditions—Plan an opening ceremony "card trick" (page 23).
   - Construct an Olympic Games flag (page 123).
   - Olympic Games Sites—Research the host city of the upcoming Olympic Games. Write a report on the interesting sights of the city that visitors may wish to see.
   - Color the flags (pages 35–37) and mount them on the world map (pages 126–127).

Planning Your Olympic Games Experience (cont.)

Class Lesson / Center Approach (cont.)

- Olympic Games Events—Using the form (page 66) research a particular sport, and each event of that sport, that is part of the Games. (Assign only one event, if preferable.)
- Olympic Games Competition—Research one or more Olympic Games stars and complete a star profile for each (page 84).

2. Set up your center only once. Include activities from each unit. For example: Report on the Greek gods, an Olympic Games sport, and/or famous Olympians, ancient and modern. Construct an Olympic Games flag, color national flags, and mount around a world map to show sites of the Olympic Games.

   Conduct your group lessons unit by unit.

Total Center Approach

Plan a period of time for each unit.

Reproduce and set up all the lessons relating to that unit, as well as additional activities (page 116) and place them at the center.

Whichever approach you use, be creative and you and your class will be enriched by your Olympic Games experience.

Where Do You Fit In?

People all over the world have favorite sports and favorite athletes. What are your favorite sports? Who are your favorite athletes?

Sports I Like to Play	Sports I Like to Watch	Is It an Olympic Sport?

My Favorite Athletes	Sports They Play	Have They Ever Been in the Olympic Games?

Olympic Games Athletes I Know	Their Sports

You are about to begin learning more about one of the world's most exciting sporting events—the Olympic Games. How much do you already know about the Olympic Games? Work together with a group of your classmates to find out more.

- Compile a list of sports that are part of the Olympic Games.
- Compile a list of athletes who have participated in past Olympic Games.
- Compile a list of athletes who are planning to participate in the next Olympic Games.
  Share your lists with your class.

Olympic Games History

36 USC 220506

The Olympic Games in Ancient Greece

For many years, the ancient Greeks gathered in the beautiful Valley of Olympia to offer sacrifices to their gods. In time, this practice came to include games and contests. These games and contests came to be known as the Olympic Games, with their first recorded date being 776 B.C. The Games were held every four years until 394 A.D. This means the ancient Olympic Games lasted more than 1000 years.

These Games, the world's oldest sports festival, became a highlight of Grecian life. All Greek male citizens were invited to participate. In time of war, temporary truces were granted. Athletes and spectators from warring Greek cities were assured safe passage to the Valley of Olympia.

Athletes and judges went to Olympia for months of training before the Games opened. They trained hard and ate well. Over six pounds of meat was not an unusual dinner for an Olympian following a day's training.

The first 13 Olympic Games featured only one event, called the *Dromos*. The Dromos was a foot race run the length of the stadium. This distance came to be known as a *stade* and was approximately 180 meters (600 feet). The stade served as the distance used to determine the basic length of future Olympic Games races, even in modern times.

The Olympic Games in Ancient Greece (cont.)

As time passed, additional events were added. Eventually, the Olympic Games became a five-day festival. From the schedule, it is evident that the Games were deeply rooted in the religion of the people.

Day one was a day of preparation. Sacrifices were made to Zeus, the king of the Greek gods. The athletes took the Olympic Games oath, swearing to compete fairly. Judges also promised to be fair and just. Competitors were assigned to the events, and a contest was held for trumpeters.

Day two opened with more sacrifices to the gods. Then came the chariot race. The low, two-wheeled chariots were drawn by four horses. Two horses were harnessed to the chariot. The other two were tethered to these horses and, as the race started, ran out in front. This race of sometimes 50 chariots was the most dangerous Olympic Games event ever held. The racers had no lanes or barriers. There were often locked wheels, overturned chariots, even head-on collisions. A somewhat calmer bareback horse race completed the morning's program. The afternoon featured the *pentathlon*. Some historians believe this was an elimination contest. Those qualifying in the long jump event went on to throw a javelin, and the four best at this ran the one-stade race. The three top runners were left for the discus throw, and the final two wrestled to the finish. Others who have studied the ancient Olympic Games believe the winner was decided after the first three events, the others having already been eliminated.

Day three opened with more religious ceremonies. Participants enjoyed a great banquet. In the afternoon, boys competed in races, boxing, and upright wrestling where the object was to throw the opponent to the ground.

Day four featured the men's running events. They ran one-stade, two-stade, and 24-stade races, races similar to those run by boys. In the afternoon, there was boxing, wrestling, and the pancratium, a savage and sometimes deadly sport that combined wrestling, boxing, and judo. The rules forbade only biting and gouging the opponent's eyes. Breaking an opponent's finger was also condemned. Athletes often forgot their oaths of good sportsmanship in their eagerness to defeat an opponent. Yet, watchful judges had their rods ready to land vigorous taps on the athletes' heads to remind them of the rules. The final event was a sprint race in armor. Runners suited up in armor to run a distance of two stades. These runners were called *hoplites*.

Day five included more sacrifices to the gods. Winners crowned with olive leaves were presented to the people. A herald would call out each person's name, the name of his proud father, and the place from which he came.

Women and girls were excluded from participating in the Olympic Games and were not allowed to watch, one reason being that the men competed nude. In time, separate races were set up for women and girls in a neighboring city. These games were known as the Herannic Games in honor of Hera, the wife of Zeus. They were held regularly, two years after each Olympic Games.

When the Roman Empire conquered Greece, the Olympic Games became less important. They ended in 394 A.D. by order of Emperor Theodosius I. In time, earthquakes, floods, and landslides buried the site of the ancient festival.

The Olympic Games in Ancient Greece (cont.)

You have read about the vigorous training of the Olympic Games athletes, including their generous appetites. One of the most famous did not settle for only six pounds of meat for his dinner. To find out more about him, follow these directions.

Reread the story of the Olympic Games in ancient Greece.

Find the missing word to complete each sentence below. Place the letter in each circle on the lines at the bottom of the page. Be sure to match your numbers correctly.

1. The early Olympic Games were held in the Valley of __ __ __ O __ __ __.

2. All Greek male __ O __ __ __ __ __ __ were invited to attend.

3. Both __ __ __ O __ __ __ __ and judges went early to train for the Games.

4. The first Olympic Games featured only one event, a __ __ O __ race.

5. During the Games, sacrifices were offered to Zeus, the king of the Greek __ O __ __ .

6. In time, the Olympic Games became a O __ __ __ -day festival.

7. The first sporting event of these festival games was the O __ __ __ __ __ __ race.

8. There was also a bareback __ __ O __ __ race.

9. The __ __ __ __ __ __ __ __ __ O __ included five events.

10. In this five-event sport, the final event was __ __ __ __ O __ __ __ .

11. Judges carried a __ O __ to enforce the rules.

12. The __ __ O __ __ __ __ events were measured in stades.

13. Runners, dressed in coats of armor, competed in the __ O __ __ __ __ __ .

14. Women were __ O __ __ __ __ __ __ from the Olympic Games.

Now it is time to find out the name of the strongest of these early Olympians and his remarkable dinner choice!

___ ___ ___ ___   ___ ___   ___ ___ ___ ___ ___ ___
1   2   3   4   5   6   7   8   9   10 11 12

ate an entire ___ ___ !
13 14

The Olympic Games in Modern Times

The site of the ancient Olympic Games lay buried until an archaeologist named Richard Chandler unearthed it in 1766. However, he was unable to pay for further excavation. In 1820, French archaeologists continued the work, uncovering the temple of Zeus. In 1875, German archaeologists started a six-year project that unearthed the entire city of Olympia. A French nobleman, Baron Pierre de Coubertin, became interested in their findings and visited the site. Coubertin loved sporting events and was fascinated by the ideals of the ancient Games. He believed that an international sports competition could promote world peace, and his efforts led to the formation of the International Olympic Games Committee.

The first modern Olympic Games were held in 1896 in Athens, Greece. Since then, with only three exceptions, they have been held every four years in different cities around the world. The exceptions have been 1916, 1940, and 1944. No Olympic Games took place in those years because of World Wars I and II.

Every effort has been made to vary the sites every four years. The 1904 Olympiad was held in St. Louis, Missouri. As boats and trains were the only means of transportation, the travel time for the majority of athletes and spectators attending was many, many days. The same held true for the 1932 Games held in Los Angeles, California. In the first half of the twentieth century, transportation to and from America was slow and expensive. Therefore, most Olympiads were held in Western Europe, where they were more easily accessible to the greatest number of athletes and spectators.

In 1900, polo was introduced, bringing horses back to the Games. Gradually, other sports and events were added. The winner's medal came to be cast in gold. These early Games included recognition of competitors in areas other than sports, and prizes were awarded in fine arts from 1912 through 1948. Today, many host cities include a festival of the fine arts which runs in conjunction with the Olympic Games.

Although figure skating and ice hockey had been events in previous Games, the first official Olympic Winter Games to feature these events was in 1924. Their scheduling brought about another change in 1992 when it was decided that the Olympic Winter Games would be held again in 1994 and every four years thereafter—1998, 2002, etc.

The Olympic Games would continue in years divisible by four 1996, 2000, etc. Having the Olympic and Olympic Winter Games in different years is a bonus for a few athletes who train for both Games and for sports fans who will be able to watch the Olympic competition every other year.

Another change over the years is the faces of the competitors. In 1900, women began to compete in lawn tennis. Archery was added for women in 1904, and swimming was included in 1912. Today women medal in almost all competitive events.

The growth of technology has also touched the Olympic Games. In 1912, the judging of race results was aided by electrical timers. In 1932, a type of electronic device was introduced, and in 1936, the Olympic Games were broadcast by radio for the first time and televised to theaters in Berlin. Televised coverage began with the 1960 Olympic Games in Rome, when images of Olympic Games events were broadcast into homes around the world. Thanks to television, people who had never heard of the Olympic Games became overnight fans, and popularity continues to grow with each competition.

The Olympic Games in Modern Times (cont.)

Male athletes were housed in their own Olympic Games village for the first time in the 1932 Games in Los Angeles. Featured were separate dining rooms for each nation, entertainment facilities, and a lounge where visitors could mingle with the athletes. Female athletes were housed in nearby hotels. Spectators gathered daily outside the Village, and a true sense of friendship existed among various nationalities.

The Olympic Games have grown in numbers of both participants and spectators. The competitions now last seventeen days. Over 2,500 athletes attended the last Olympic Winter Games. They competed for gold, silver, and bronze medals in more than 50 events. More than 10,000 athletes attended the Olympic Games in 1992. They competed for gold, silver, and bronze medals in more than 250 events. There are 200 nations that have Olympic Games committees.

There have been some rocky moments in the history of the Olympic Games. For example, the Games of 1936 in Berlin, Germany, collided with politics in the form of German Nazi leader Adolph Hitler. Despite boycott threats from American Jews justifiably angered by Hitler's outrageous policies, the Olympic Games went ahead as planned. Hitler certainly had not planned on the participation of American track superstar, Jesse Owens, the supposedly "inferior" African-American, who raced to four gold medals—and international acclaim—in Berlin. In 1972, at the Olympic Games in Munich, West Germany, a terrorist attack marred the competition. Arab terrorists held as hostages, and then killed, 11 athletes from the Israeli Olympic Games Team. Years later, a terrorist bomb forced the closing of Centennial Park at the Atlanta Games in 1996.

At times, countries have boycotted the Games because of opposing political views. A major Olympic Games boycott occurred in 1980 when the United States led several nations in staying away from the Moscow Games. This was to protest the Soviet Union's invasion of Afghanistan. In 1984, the Soviets led a boycott of the Los Angeles Games in an attempt to get even. Both boycotts hurt the athletes who had trained for many years and could not compete. Since then, there has been a positive change in world events. The future for full attendance at upcoming Olympic Games looks hopeful.

In spite of all the changes, the ideals of the Olympic Games are the same. They are held in the hope of promoting world peace, understanding, and fair and friendly athletic competition.

Modern Olympic Games Time Line

Below you will see some dates that are significant in the development of the modern Olympic Games. Some dates reflect technological changes in presenting the Olympic Games. Other dates reflect politics and its affect on team participation. Write an important event in the history of the Games in the box above each date.

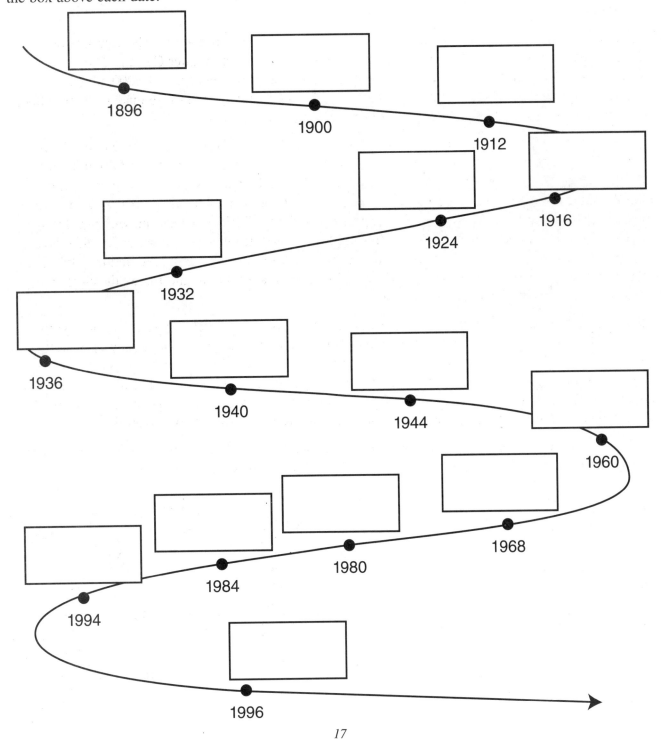

Olympic Games: Ancient and Modern

Use the diagram below to compare and contrast the facts unique to the ancient and modern Games.

In the circle on the top, write the facts unique to the ancient Games. In the circle on the bottom, write the facts unique to the modern Games. In the area where the circles intersect, write the facts true of both Games.

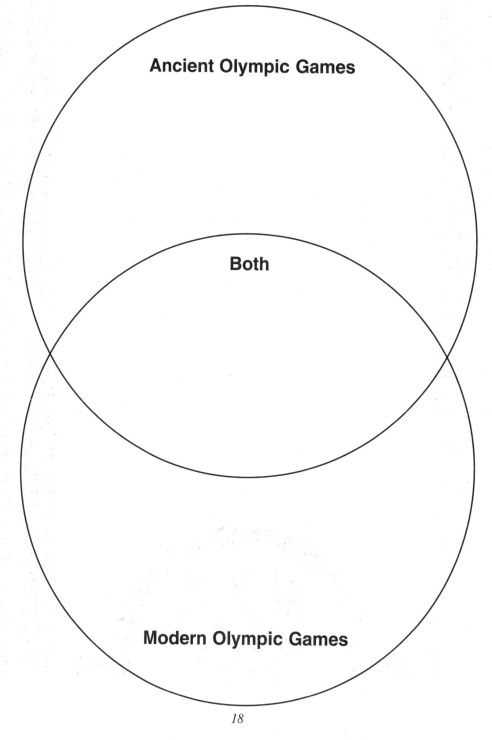

Ancient Olympic Games

Both

Modern Olympic Games

Olympic Games
Traditions

Olympism

Olympism*, the philosophy of the Olympic Movement, was developed by Pierre de Coubertin. It is a set of values that enhance the physical, intellectual, and spiritual growth of participants through sport, art, and music while promoting friendship and understanding in the world.

Olympism offers the athlete:

- physical and moral development because of the exercise involved and the discipline and control over mind and body required during training and competition.

- an attitude of respect for competitors of other nations.

- an appreciation of the beauty of movement that can be transferred into other areas of culture.

Students will:

- define the idea of Olympism and apply the values inherent in the Olympic Movement to their daily lives.

- determine that winning is not the most important part of the Olympic Games.

- differentiate between a professional and an amateur athlete.

- recognize that the reward athletes receive for winning events in the Olympic Games is a gold, silver, or bronze medal—with no monetary prize.

- explore the impact of political differences on the Olympic Games.

- recognize that the use of banned substances is contrary to the philosophy of Olympism.

- develop an appreciation for the cultural differences among Olympic athletes.

*USOC. Olympism: A Basic Guide to History, Ideas, and Sports of the Olympic Movement. Griffin Publishing, 1996

Opening and Closing Ceremonies

Opening Ceremonies

In ancient Greece, the first day of Olympic Games competition opened with judges in royal purple robes, a heralder, and a trumpeter entering the Hippodrome, the oval track used for the races. The judges took their stand and the competitors, in chariots drawn by four prancing horses, paraded past them. The herald called out each competitor's name, the name of his father, and his city. Then the herald declared the Games officially open.

More than 2,500 years later, on a cool afternoon in 1896, another opening ceremony took place. Parading into the stadium in Athens, Greece, were 258 athletes from 13 different countries. Along with the 70,000 spectators in the stands, they heard the King of Greece declare the Games of the first modern Olympiad officially open.

The opening ceremonies have continued as a grand highlight of the Olympic Games. With television carrying its imagery around the world, the pageantry has grown. Each host city stages a spectacular performance of music, dance, and special effects. Local citizens, young and old, perform together to welcome the world to their city.

Athletes from each participating country parade into the stadium, following their national flag. Each flag is carried by the athlete chosen by his or her teammates to lead the delegation. As each team passes the reviewing stand, the flagbearer dips the flag in honor of the head of state of the host country.

However, you may note that the flag of the United States is never lowered. This practice goes back to the London Olympic Games of 1908. In decorating the stadium for the Games, the organizers forgot to display the flags of some of the participating nations, including the United States. One country withdrew its team from the Olympic Games in protest. The United States decided to stay and compete. Yet, they did not allow the slight to go unnoticed. At the opening ceremonies, the flagbearer held the banner high as the team passed in front of the King of England. Since that time, flagbearers of the United States have refused to lower the flag for any head of state. Athletes from Greece are always given the honor of entering the stadium first. They are followed in alphabetical order by athletes of the other countries. The host country's team enters last.

A representative of the host country welcomes the athletes and declares the Games officially open. The athletes then recite the Olympic Games oath. A flock of doves—the birds symbolic of peace—is usually released, and the Olympic Games flame is lit. The ceremonies usually conclude with an explosion of breathtaking fireworks.

Opening and Closing Ceremonies (cont.)

Closing Ceremonies

After sixteen days of intense athletic competition, the setting of new world records, and the winning or losing of medals by the world's best athletes, the Olympic Games playing fields fall silent. As in the beginning, these Olympic Games athletes gather together for a ceremonial goodbye. This spectacular event is the closing ceremony of the Olympic Games. The athletes enter the stadium one last time to say good-bye to their fans, congratulate the winners, and celebrate the Olympic Games experience. The athletes are seen entering the stadium walking side by side, celebrating their new friendships, many times with competitors from other countries.

As the athletes gather together, representatives from the host country share parting thoughts of the Olympic Games. The flag from the country hosting the next Olympic Games is raised, and representatives from that country are invited to the podium, where they invite the world to their country for the next Olympic Games. Finally, the Olympic Games are declared officially closed, the Olympic Games flame is extinguished, and the Olympic Games flag is lowered. Following this emotional ceremony, there is a variety of entertainment, and once again the night sky explodes with fireworks.

Activity

Host cities begin to plan their spectacular opening and closing ceremonies years in advance. Watch videos of past festivities, then divide your class into groups to plan new ceremonies. Let them present their plans—complete with visuals and music—to an Olympic Games Planning Committee for review.

Designing a Card Trick

Now that you have read about the opening and closing ceremonies of the Olympic Games, you may enjoy participating in some of the fun. In many recent Olympic Games, the fans have been included in the show. When reaching their seats inside the stadium, spectators have found colored cards taped to their seats. At a given signal, the spectators hold up the cards, and the blend of colors presents a special picture or message. It takes a great deal of planning to coordinate these "card tricks." Color the card trick below. 1=blue, 2=black, 3=red, 4=green. When you have finished the numbers, color the background yellow.

Directions: Use a sheet of graph paper (page 136) to plan a card trick for one section of your Olympic Games stadium. First, write a message or, better yet, draw a picture. Your lines must stay on the graph lines so you will have squared figures. When you have finished drawing your pattern, color it.

Grid pattern (each character is one grid square; blank squares are spaces):

```
         1111 1111
         1    1  1
         1    1  1
         1 11 1  1
         1  1 1  1
         1  1 1  1
         1111 1111


2222 2  2 2222 3333 3 3 3333
2    2  2 2  2  33  3 3 3
2    2  2 2  2  33  3 3 3
222  2  2 2222  33  333 333
2    2  2 22    33  3 3 3
2    2  2 2 2   33  3 3 3
2    2222 2  2  33  3 3 3333


   4444 4444 4   444
   4    4  4 4   4  4
   4    4  4 4   4  4
   4 44 4  4 4   4  4
   4  4 4  4 4   4  4
   4  4 4  4 4   4  4
   4444 4444 444 444
```

The Olympic Games Symbol

The five rings, the familiar symbol of the Olympic Games, were discovered by archaeologists. They found them engraved on an altar uncovered during the excavation at Delphi, Greece. It has been suggested that they were used as a symbol of the Olympic Games in ancient Greece though their significance is debated.

Baron Pierre de Coubertin, who helped initiate the modern Olympic Games, used the rings to symbolize the participating continents of the world. These probably included North and South America (counted as one), Europe, Asia, Africa, and Australia. He chose the colors blue, yellow, black, green, and red because the flag of each competing nation has at least one of these colors on it.

The colored rings placed on a background of white became the design for the Olympic Games flag. Although displayed in Paris, France, a few years before, it was first flown at the Olympic Games in Antwerp, Belgium, in 1920. Since then, it has been raised at the opening ceremonies of each successive Olympic Games.

Working in a group with four of your classmates, use the ring pattern on page 124 to construct a large Olympic Games flag.

The Olympic Games Oath

At each opening ceremony since 1920, a representative of the host country has led the athletes in reciting the Olympic Games oath. The Olympic Games oath is a promise to compete fairly. The words may vary from Olympic Games to Olympic Games, but the spirit remains the same.

Here are the words of the oath:

> *In the name of all competitors, I promise that we shall take part in these Olympic Games, respecting and abiding by the rules which govern them, in the true spirit of sportsmanship, for the glory of sport and the honor of our teams.*

1. Why is it important to follow the rules of a sport?

   _____

   _____

   _____

2. What is the "true spirit of sportsmanship"?

   _____

   _____

   _____

3. What are the goals of Olympic Games competition, according to the oath? What do the goals mean?

   _____

   _____

   _____

4. Work in small groups to write a new "Olympic Games oath" for your class to use when competing in sporting events.

   _____

   _____

   _____

   _____

   _____

The Olympic Games Torch

The lighting of the Olympic Games flame marks the climax of each opening ceremony. This practice can be traced back to the Olympic Games of the ancient Greeks. There, the priests placed sacrifices on an altar and prepared to set them on fire. Some 200 meters away, a group of young Grecian boys waited for the signal to start their foot race. The winning runner seized the flaming torch from the priest's hand and lit the sacrificial fire.

The tradition of lighting an Olympic Games torch in Olympia, Greece, has been a part of the modern Olympic Games for many years. Several weeks before the opening of each Olympic Games, the flaming torch begins its journey over land and sea to the site of the competition. Once it reaches the host country, a series of runners carry it in relays to the Olympic Games site. It is a very special honor to be one of these runners.

At the opening ceremonies of the Olympic Games, the torch is carried into the stadium. It is then passed to the final runner, an honored citizen of the host country, often a former Olympian. He or she then climbs the stairs to the top of the stadium and tilts the torch to light the large flame that will burn throughout the Olympic Games. At the 1992 Olympic Games in Barcelona, an archer shot a lit arrow at the Olympic cauldron, hitting the target perfectly to light the torch.

Since the first torch was carried by relay runners to the Berlin Games of 1936, Olympic Games torches have made lengthy and interesting journeys to the Game sites. Here are the stories of a few of their trips.

In 1948, the torch made the journey of 186 miles (300 km) from Olympia to London, England, in 12 days. It was carried mostly by runners and crossed the English Channel on a warship of the Royal Navy.

In 1956, 3,500 torchbearers participated in a run from Olympia to Athens, Greece. There, the flame was put into a miner's lamp and flown to Cairns, Australia. From there it went on to Sydney and finally to the Game site of Melbourne. Australia is a big continent, and the distance covered on that land alone was 2,825 miles (4,545 km). It took 2,830 runners 13 days and nights to complete the journey.

In 1968, the torch was carried first from Greece to Spain. There it was put aboard a ship that followed the route of Columbus to the New World. It finally reached its destination of Mexico City in time for the Olympic Games.

The most spectacular torch run probably took place in 1960. Walt Disney was called upon to stage the opening ceremonies at Squaw Valley, California. His plan included flying the Olympic Games torch from Olympia to Los Angeles by jet. There it was taken to the Los Angeles Coliseum, site of the 1932 Opening Ceremonies. It was met by 600 high school athletes who each ran a mile through California cities to the foot of the hills of Squaw Valley. Then, a helicopter lifted the torch to the top of the ski slope where a skier waited to race it down the mountain. He passed it to a champion speed skater who carried it for a final lap around the stadium oval before lighting the flame. Despite a blinding snowstorm on opening day, all went according to plan. The flame burned brightly for the 16 days of those Olympic Winter Games.

The Olympic Games Torch (cont.)

Now it is your turn to carry the torch. Use the world map on pages 126–127 to trace the route of the torch from Olympia, Greece, to each of the sites on page 26. Use a different color to mark each route.

Choose another color to trace the route of the torch from Olympia to the site of the most recent Olympic Games. Use the map scale to approximate how far it traveled.

Suppose you were chosen to be the final runner to carry the torch to light the Olympic Games flame. Write a newspaper article about your big day.

Fill the outline of the torch (page 125) with words that you believe represent the spirit of the Olympic Games.

Example:

The Olympic Games Motto

The Olympic Games motto is written in Latin, the language of the ancient Roman Empire: "Citius, Altius, Fortius." In English, these three words are "Swifter, Higher, Stronger." Written by Father Henri Didon, headmaster of the Aucueil School near Paris, France, the motto represents the athletic ideal of the Olympic Games.

Directions: In the space below, create an artistic version of the Olympic Games motto using either the Latin or English words. You may wish to use special lettering, calligraphy, a picture of an athlete, or another Olympic Games symbol.

Catching Pin Fever

If you have the opportunity to attend an Olympic Games, you will find that pin fever is a contagious "disease." Even for those exposed only through television, pin fever is caught quite easily. In fact, the epidemic has led to its becoming one of the world's fastest spreading hobbies.

Commemorative pins have been issued to celebrate Olympic Games for many years. However, for most Americans, major pin collecting began in 1984 when Los Angeles hosted the Olympic Games. Every day, visitors gathered around the Olympic Games village sites, mingling with athletes and other visitors to trade pins. Even during sporting events, spectators often stole time to scan the pins displayed on the caps of those around them. Then, during a break in the competition, they would conclude their trades.

The International Olympic Games Committee (IOC) controls the licensing to manufacture and distribute Olympic Games pins. Only those approved by the IOC may display the five-ring symbol on the pin. This symbol must be there for the pin to be considered "official."

With each Olympic Games come several varieties of pins. Each country strikes a team pin. These are distributed to the athletes to trade or offer in friendship to other competitors. United States athletes also are given pins representing their individual sports.

The host city issues pins. There are many varieties. Some show the logo of the Olympic Games. Others show the Olympic Games' mascot in a variety of poses. A set may be designed showing the mascot carrying a flag of each nation or competing in featured events. A pin may also be issued by the Olympic Games committee of an individual country. Since 1984, corporations or businesses have sponsored and helped pay for the Olympic Games. Pins are issued by these official sponsors. If you enjoy collecting, perhaps you can visit a pin show in your area and see some of the pins for yourself. You just may become infected with pin fever! Meanwhile, look over some of the drawings of past Olympic Games pins on this page. Then on page 30, create a design for an Olympic Games pin of your own.

Catching Pin Fever (cont.)

Directions: Design a pin that can be used for the upcoming Olympic Games.

Awarding of Olympic Games Medals

The awarding of wreaths and medals has been a part of the Olympic Games since its inception. In ancient Greece, the olive branch or wreath represented the highest honor one could receive for winning an Olympic Games event. As the wreath was presented, a herald would shout the name of the victor, the name of his father, and the name of his country. No other prizes or awards were given at the games. However, when the victor returned home, he often received money, property, had a street named after him, and, occasionally, an ode would be written in his honor.

In 1896, the first Olympic Games of the modern era were held. Instead of receiving olive wreaths, Olympic Games champions were awarded gold, silver, or bronze medals. Today, Olympic Games champions receive their medals during momentous ceremonies. Gold, silver, and bronze medalists stand at attention on podiums with their countries' flags behind them as they listen to the anthem from the gold medalist's country. This truly is the most treasured prize in amateur sports. Jesse Owens said, "If you don't try to win, you might as well hold the Olympic Games in somebody's back yard." Baron Pierre de Coubertin, father of the modern Olympic Games said, "The most important thing in the Olympic Games is not to win but to take part, just as the most important thing in life is not the triumph but the struggle. The essential thing is not to have conquered but to have fought well." Taking part in the Olympic Games is truly an honor, but winning a medal is every participant's dream.

Activity

Medals are designed anew for each Olympic Games and even differ between winter and summer. Have your students create medals for first (gold), second (silver), and third (bronze) place using the medal patterns on page 121.

Olympic Games Sites

36 USC 220506

Host Cities

Summer		Winter
Year	**City/Country**	**City/Country**
1896	Athens, Greece	***
1900	Paris, France	***
1904	St. Louis, MO, USA	***
1908	London, England	***
1912	Stockholm, Sweden	***
1916	Not Held (World War I)	***
1920	Antwerp, Belgium	***
1924	Paris, France	Chamonix, France
1928	Amsterdam, The Netherlands	St. Moritz, Switzerland
1932	Los Angeles, CA, USA	Lake Placid, NY, USA
1936	Berlin, Germany	Garmisch-Partenkirchen, Germany
1940	Not Held (World War II)	Not Held (World War II)
1944	Not Held (World War II)	Not Held (World War II)
1948	London, England	St. Moritz, Switzerland
1952	Helsinki, Finland	Oslo, Norway
1956	Melbourne, Australia	Cortina, Italy
1960	Rome, Italy	Squaw Valley, CA, USA
1964	Tokyo, Japan	Innsbruck, Austria
1968	Mexico City, Mexico	Grenoble, France
1972	Munich, West Germany	Sapporo, Japan
1976	Montreal, Canada	Innsbruck, Austria
1980	Moscow, Russia	Lake Placid, NY, USA
1984	Los Angeles, CA, USA	Sarajevo, Yugoslavia
1988	Seoul, South Korea	Calgary, Canada
1992	Barcelona, Spain	Albertville, France
1996	Atlanta, GA, USA	1994 Lillehammer, Norway
2000	Sydney, Australia	1998 Nagano, Japan
2004	Athens, Greece	2002 Salt Lake City, UT, USA

*** Olympic Winter Games began in 1924.

Here Comes the USA

On the following pages (35–37) you will find the flags of Olympic Games host countries where U.S. athletes participated.

- Use a reference book to identify and color the flags.

- Write the name of the country and date(s) of its Olympic Games on the line below each flag.

- Color the frame of each flag that flew over the Olympic Winter Games blue and the frame of each flag that flew over the Olympic Games red.

- Use the blank to fill in the next Olympic Games location.

- Locate and color these host countries on the world map (pages 126–127).

- Mount the world map on a larger sheet of paper 16" x 24" (40.5 cm x 61 cm).

- Arrange and paste the flags around the world map.

- Use your ruler to draw a line from the flag to its country.

Here Comes the USA (cont.)

Olympic Winter Games

1. _____

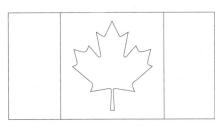

2. _____

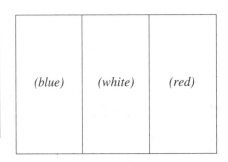

3. _____

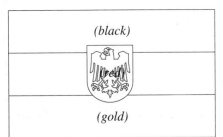

(black)

(gold)

4. _____

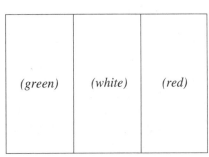

(green) (white) (red)

5. _____

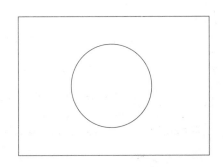

6. _____

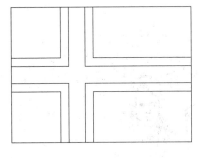

7. _____

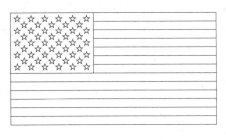

8. _____

(blue)

(white)

(red)

9. _____

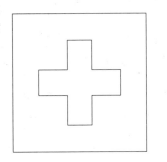

10. _____

11. _____

12. _____

Here Comes the USA (cont.)

Olympic Games

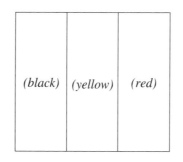

(black) (yellow) (red)

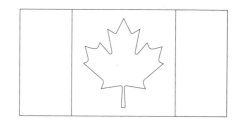

1. _____

2. _____

3. _____

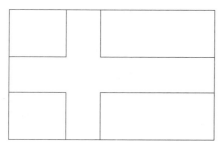

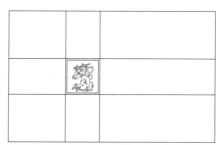

(blue) (white) (red)

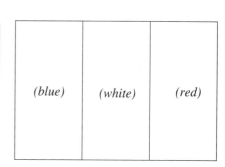

4. _____

5. _____

6. _____

(black)

(gold)

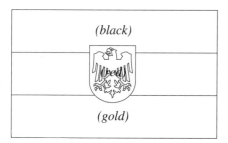

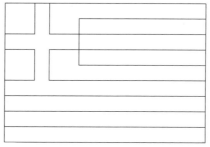

(green) (white) (red)

7. _____

8. _____

9. _____

Here Comes the USA (cont.)

Olympic Games

10. _____

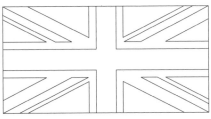

(red)

(white)

(blue)

11. _____

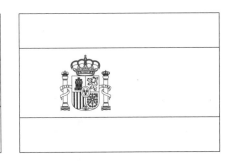

12. _____

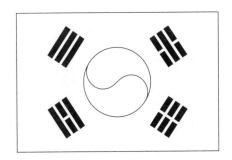

13. _____

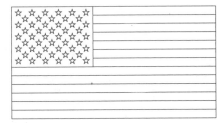

14. _____

15. _____

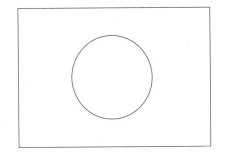

16. _____

(white)

(blue)

(red)

17. _____

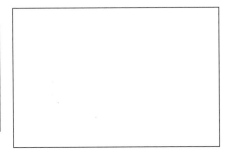

18. _____

Looking Over the Logos

The five entwined rings is the recognized symbol of the Olympic Games. Yet, each of the Olympic Games has its own symbol, as well.

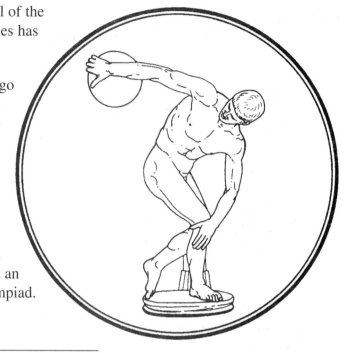

Even though its origin is in modern times, the logo of the discus thrower is the recognized symbol for the ancient games. The discus was unique to the Greeks. The tossing of it, along with the javelin, grew out of the hurling of stones and sticks in ancient times. The discus thrower is representative of all the strength and power of an Olympian.

Directions: Color the logo of the discus thrower. Then use your imagination to write a story about an ancient Grecian discus thrower and his first Olympiad.

_____

_____

_____

_____

_____

_____

_____

The city of Atlanta, Georgia, chose the centennial torch for its logo for the 1996 Olympic Games. The handle was designed to resemble an ancient Greek column, alluding to the Greek origin of the ancient Olympic Games as well as marking the 100th anniversary of the modern Olympiad. The flame on the torch changes into stars, representing the athletic ambition of each Olympian.

In 1994, the representatives of the city of Lillehammer, Norway, explained their logo as symbolic of the northern lights, a natural phenomenon unique to far northern countries such as Norway and the symbol of winter, depicting the power and drama of the Olympic Games.

Logo Match

Here are some logos used in past Olympic Games. Using the clues provided, see whether you can match each of the host cities listed below with the logo of its Games. Some of the logos may be used more than once.

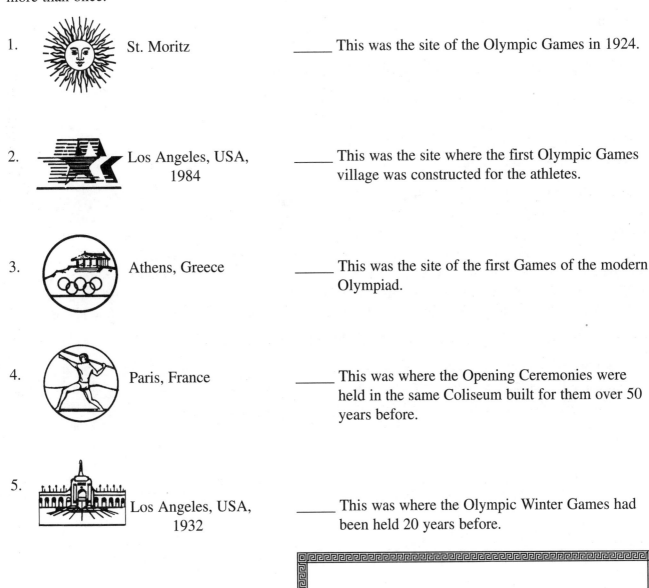

1.   St. Moritz

_____ This was the site of the Olympic Games in 1924.

2.   Los Angeles, USA, 1984

_____ This was the site where the first Olympic Games village was constructed for the athletes.

3.   Athens, Greece

_____ This was the site of the first Games of the modern Olympiad.

4.   Paris, France

_____ This was where the Opening Ceremonies were held in the same Coliseum built for them over 50 years before.

5.   Los Angeles, USA, 1932

_____ This was where the Olympic Winter Games had been held 20 years before.

Choose the city of a past or current Games or a city where you would like to see the Olympic Games one day. Design a logo for these Games. Include the name of the city, the year, and the Olympic Games rings on your logo.

Choosing a Mascot

When a city is awarded the Olympic Games, the organizing committee begins to think about choosing a mascot. It needs to be representative of both the host city and country. This mascot will appear on posters and pins. It will "come alive" as a costumed character to add its welcome to the opening ceremonies. Its animated features will add charm and enjoyment to every part of the Games. It is hoped its use in advertising will also bring in revenue to help pay for staging the various events.

While you may be familiar with the mascots of recent Olympic Games, you may not be familiar with those of earlier Olympic Games. Let's meet some of them now.

The first official mascot made its appearance at Munich in 1972. The Germans chose a typically German dog, a dachshund. They named him Waldi. The inspiration for Waldi came from a real-life, long-haired dachshund of a championship line, a dog named Cherie von Birkenhof.

Possibly the most popular of U.S. mascots was Sam the Eagle, the choice of the Los Angeles Olympic Games in 1984. Consideration first was given to choosing a mascot representative of the sun and palm trees of Southern California, perhaps a seal. The bear, the state symbol, was also considered. Finally, the committee decided on the eagle. Not only was it the national bird of the United States, but it represented the Olympic Games motto as well. Indeed, the eagle was swifter, higher, stronger! The final design selected was the work of an artist from Walt Disney Productions. He changed the usually stern-looking bird into the warm and friendly Sam. As he was pictured competing in various events, his wings were drawn as arms and his feathers as fingers.

Another popular mascot was Hodori, the tiger cub featured at the 1988 Seoul Games. The tiger is a helpful, friendly figure in Korean art and legend. His name was chosen from among 2,295 ideas suggested by the public. "Ho" is Korean for tiger, and "dori" is a suffix meaning little. He was designed standing on two feet, wearing the Olympic Games rings about his neck. On his head was a traditional farmer's hat with a streamer spiraling above in an "S" for Seoul.

Other animals that have been part of the Olympic Games include a bear named Misha at Moscow in 1980, and a sheepdog named Cobi, the friendly greeter at Barcelona in 1992.

The polar bear cubs, Hidy and Howdy, gave a warm welcome to visitors to the 1988 Olympic Winter Games in Calgary. This brother and sister team were the first double mascots selected. Sporting colorful costumes, they were quite representative of the flavor of western Canada. Likewise, their names, selected from over 7,000 entries, expressed typical western greetings.

Another mascot pair made an appearance at Lillehammer in 1994. Named after a prince and princess of the 13th century, Kristin and Hakon were chosen to represent the happy children of modern Norway.

The mascots for the 1998 Games in Nagano, Japan, were four owls called Snowlets.

The three mascots for the Sydney 2000 Games are Syd, a platypus, Millie, an echidna, and Olly, a kookaburra.

Choosing a Mascot (cont.)

Other Olympic Games and Olympic Winter Games' mascots have reflected equal creativity. Roni the raccoon, whose mask-like face suggested the goggles and caps of a skier, welcomed the athletes to Lake Placid in 1980. In 1984, Sarajevo chose a wolf named Vucko, meaning "wandering Olympic Games ambassador." The Albertville mascot in 1992 was Magique, a jack-in-the-box imp designed to delight the children of the world.

Few pictures exist of Waldi, the first Olympic Games mascot. However, we know he had a light blue head and tail. His body was painted in vertical stripes, using at least three of the Olympic Games colors. The Olympic Games rings were also included. It was ruled that mascots must be at least 5 inches (13 cm) long so that they could easily be seen. Using this description, produce your own version of Waldi participating in an event or holding a flag.

Waldi

Choosing a Mascot (cont.)

Draw and color a new mascot for a future Olympic Games or Winter Olympic Games. Name your mascot and tell why it would be a suitable choice. Write a story about this future star of the Olympic Games.

Postermania

Once a host city is selected for an Olympic Games, the committee in charge of arrangements sets out to design a poster. They try to combine the symbols of the Olympic Games with the logo of the Olympic Games, and add the flavor of their city.

Below are some posters from past Olympic Games. Choose a city of an upcoming (or past) Olympic Games and on a separate piece of paper, design your own poster.

See the Sites

Each Olympic Games draws many visitors, all eager to watch their favorite sports. In addition to watching the Olympic Games, visitors always want to spend time getting to know the host city.

Pretend that you run a travel agency. Choose the site of a past or future Olympic Games. Your assignment is to create a brochure describing the historical, cultural, and entertainment attractions available to visitors.

Fold your brochure to create a cover. Make illustrations that will encourage visitors to want to come to your city's Olympic Games. Use a reference book to complete the information below. Add this information to your brochure.

We invite you to visit _____, _____.

We are proud of our city and hope you will enjoy your visit here.

Since you will be coming in _____, when the daytime temperature will be about _____, you may want to bring along _____ clothing. At night, it falls to _____, so you may need _____.

Our city was founded in _____ by _____.

Interesting historical landmarks include

_____

_____

There are many cultural spots to visit, including

_____

_____

No visitor to our city wants to miss seeing _____.

This is a very special attraction because _____

_____

Entertainment attractions include _____.

Be sure you do not miss _____ because _____

_____

Our city is also very proud of _____

_____

Thank you for choosing to visit us. We hope your stay here will be a pleasant one.

Olympic Disciplines, Events and Sports

USA

36 USC 220506

Olympic Disciplines, Events, and Sports

The International Olympic Committee chooses the disciplines, events, and sports for each Olympic Games.

- *Disciplines* are a branch of an Olympic sport comprising one or several events.

- *Events* are competitions in an Olympic sport or in one of the disciplines. (The number of events can change each year depending on program approval by the IOC.)

- An Olympic *sport* is widely practiced by men in at least seventy-five countries and on four continents, and by women in at least forty countries and on three continents. Sports widely practiced in at least twenty-five countries and on three continents may be included in the program of the Olympic Winter Games. Some sports have many separate events (athletics, swimming, gymnastics). Other sports, such as volleyball have one; the game is the event.

After 1992, the Olympic Winter Games and the Olympic Games were no longer held within the same calendar year. Olympic Winter Games were next held in 1994, after only a two-year interval, and every four years thereafter. The Olympic Games were scheduled for 1996, and every four years thereafter.

In the past, the host country was allowed to include one or two demonstration sports. For example, baseball and tennis were demonstration sports in Los Angeles in 1984 and became medal sports in the 1988 Games. Curling, a team game played on ice, became an official sport for men and women in 1998.

Olympic Games

Aquatics (44)
    Diving (8)
    Swimming (32)
    Synchronized Swimming (2)
    Water Polo (2)
Archery (4)
Athletics (Track and Field) (46)
Badminton (5)
Baseball (1)
Basketball (2)
Boxing (12)
Canoe/Kayak (16)

Cycling (18)
Equestrian (6)
Fencing (10)
Field Hockey (2)
Gymnastics (18)
Judo (14)
Modern Pentathlon (2)
Rowing (14)
Sailing/Yachting (11)
Shooting (17)
Soccer (Football) (2)
Softball (1)

Table Tennis (4)
Taekwondo (8)
Team Handball (2)
Tennis (4)
Triathlon (2)
Volleyball (4)
Weightlifting (15)
Wrestling (16)
    Freestyle (8)
    Greco-Roman (8)

Olympic Winter Games

Biathlon (6)
Bobsled (2), Women's events will soon be added.
Curling (2)
Figure Skating (4)
    Singles (2)
    Pairs (1)
    Dance (1)

Hockey (2)
Luge (3)
Skiing (33)
    Alpine (10)
    Combined (2)
    Freestyle (4)
    Nordic (10)
    Ski Jumping (3)
    Snowboarding (4)

Speed Skating (16)
    Long Track (10)
    Short Track (6)

Summer Events Jigsaw

The cards on the following pages contain the names, symbols, and descriptions of Olympic Games summer events.

Directions: Cut out all the cards, then match each sporting event with its description. The cards are designed so that you will know when you have it right. If you wish, you may glue your completed cards onto a large sheet of paper.

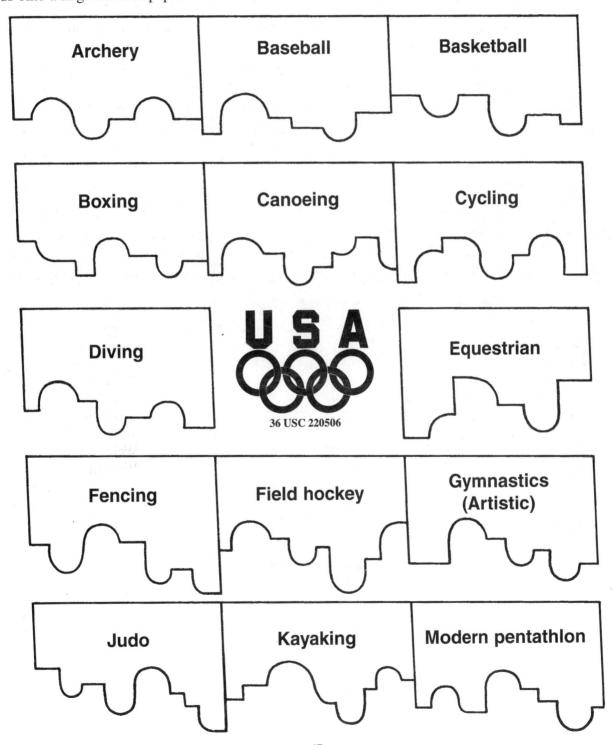

Summer Events Jigsaw (cont.)

Directions: Cut out and match each sporting event with its description.

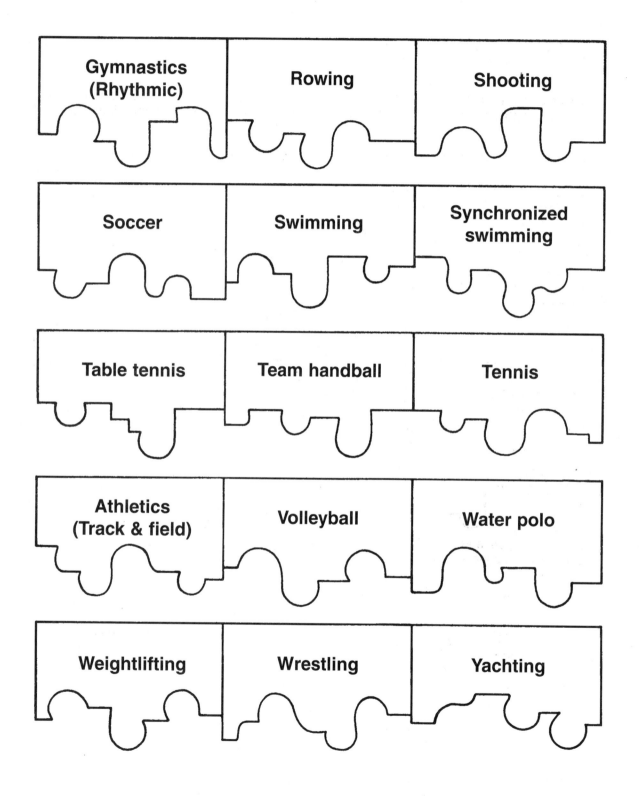

Summer Events Jigsaw (cont.)

Directions: Cut out and match each description with its sport.

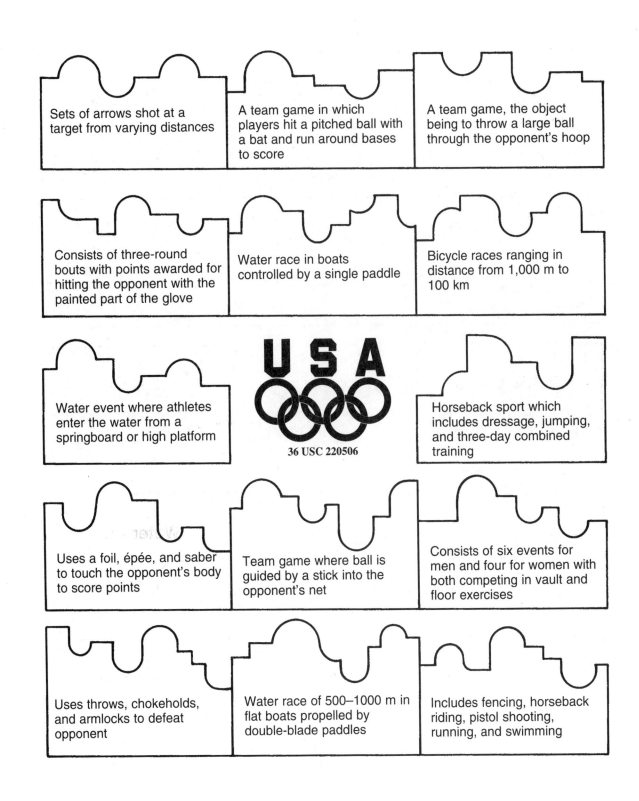

Sets of arrows shot at a target from varying distances

A team game in which players hit a pitched ball with a bat and run around bases to score

A team game, the object being to throw a large ball through the opponent's hoop

Consists of three-round bouts with points awarded for hitting the opponent with the painted part of the glove

Water race in boats controlled by a single paddle

Bicycle races ranging in distance from 1,000 m to 100 km

Water event where athletes enter the water from a springboard or high platform

USA
36 USC 220506

Horseback sport which includes dressage, jumping, and three-day combined training

Uses a foil, épée, and saber to touch the opponent's body to score points

Team game where ball is guided by a stick into the opponent's net

Consists of six events for men and four for women with both competing in vault and floor exercises

Uses throws, chokeholds, and armlocks to defeat opponent

Water race of 500–1000 m in flat boats propelled by double-blade paddles

Includes fencing, horseback riding, pistol shooting, running, and swimming

Summer Events Jigsaw (cont.)

Directions: Cut out and match each description with its sport.

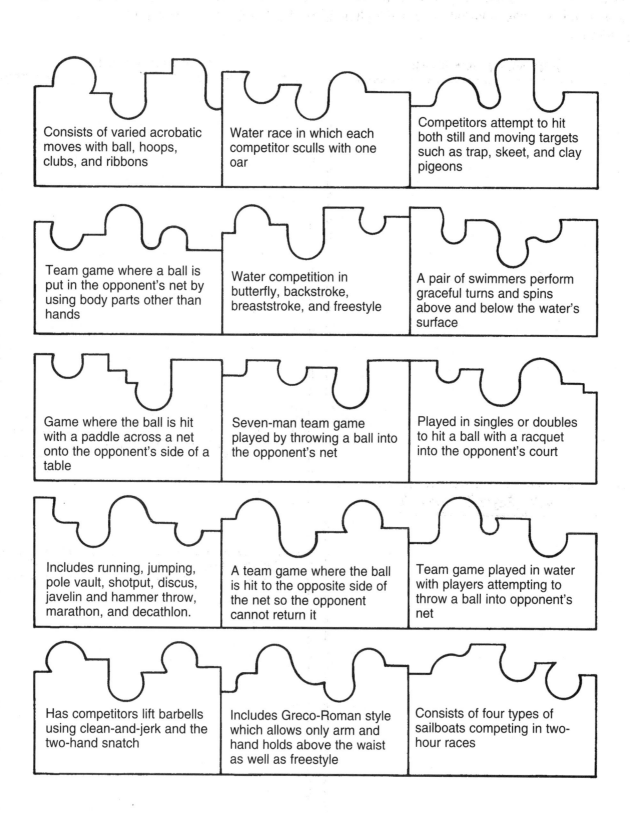

Consists of varied acrobatic moves with ball, hoops, clubs, and ribbons

Water race in which each competitor sculls with one oar

Competitors attempt to hit both still and moving targets such as trap, skeet, and clay pigeons

Team game where a ball is put in the opponent's net by using body parts other than hands

Water competition in butterfly, backstroke, breaststroke, and freestyle

A pair of swimmers perform graceful turns and spins above and below the water's surface

Game where the ball is hit with a paddle across a net onto the opponent's side of a table

Seven-man team game played by throwing a ball into the opponent's net

Played in singles or doubles to hit a ball with a racquet into the opponent's court

Includes running, jumping, pole vault, shotput, discus, javelin and hammer throw, marathon, and decathlon.

A team game where the ball is hit to the opposite side of the net so the opponent cannot return it

Team game played in water with players attempting to throw a ball into opponent's net

Has competitors lift barbells using clean-and-jerk and the two-hand snatch

Includes Greco-Roman style which allows only arm and hand holds above the waist as well as freestyle

Consists of four types of sailboats competing in two-hour races

Summer Events Recall

How many events from the Olympic Games can you recall? You may wish to use the cards which you have assembled or test your memory in completing the lists below. Your "target number" is in parentheses.

Events using a ball (12)

Events using a net (8)

Events on horseback (2)

Events played in water (9)

Events needing no special equipment (7)

Summer Events Recall (cont.)

Events with throwing (11)

Athletics (Track & field) events (13)

Events covering long distances (6)

Team events (8)

Events with kicking (3)

It is also fun to do this activity as a timed challenge for an individual or a team.

Summer Events Crossword

If you know your summer events, you will be able to solve this crossword in record Olympic Games time!

Across

1. In _____, athletes use a racquet to compete.

6. _____ is a team sport combining basketball and soccer, and is played in a pool.

8. In the sport of _____, a birdie is hit back and forth across a net.

10. The _____ participated in the sport of basketball.

12. In the sport of _____, one competes on the uneven parallel bars.

13. _____ is a sport for people who are not afraid of heights.

Down

2. The individual medley is a race in _____.

3. The decathalon combines ten ___ & _____ events.

4. A _____ is used when competing in fencing.

5. A coxswain steers a boat in the sport of _____.

7. _____ was a spectator sport in Atlanta in 1996.

9. An _____ is achieved when the ball is served past the opposing team and remains in bounds.

11. Four runners together make up a _____.

12. Mark Spitz won seven _____ medals during the 1972 Olympic Games.

Winter Events Jigsaw

The cards on the following pages contain the names, symbols, and descriptions of Winter Game events.

Directions: Cut out all the cards, then match each sporting event with its description. The cards are designed so that you will know when you have it right. If you wish, you may glue your completed cards onto a large sheet of paper.

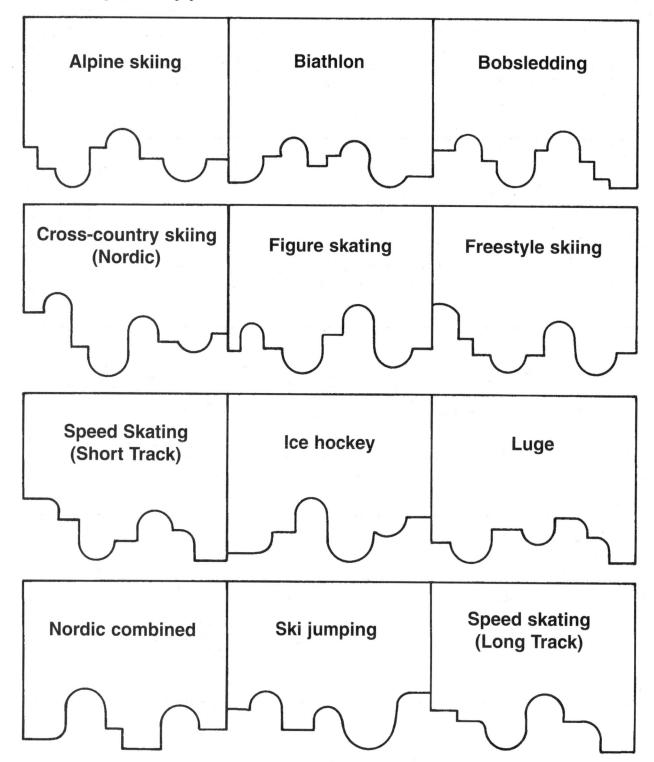

Winter Events Jigsaw (cont.)

Directions: Cut out and match each description with its sport.

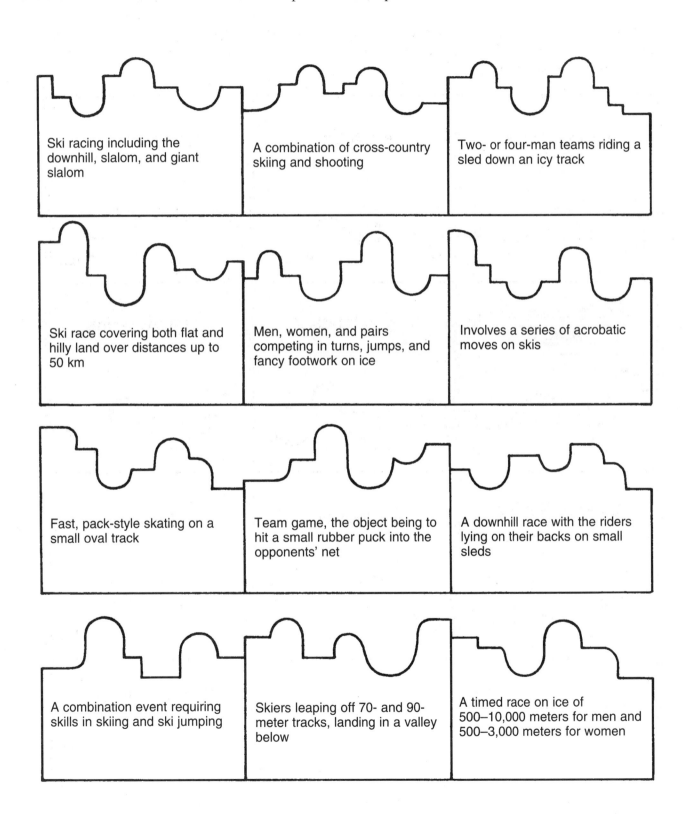

Ski racing including the downhill, slalom, and giant slalom

A combination of cross-country skiing and shooting

Two- or four-man teams riding a sled down an icy track

Ski race covering both flat and hilly land over distances up to 50 km

Men, women, and pairs competing in turns, jumps, and fancy footwork on ice

Involves a series of acrobatic moves on skis

Fast, pack-style skating on a small oval track

Team game, the object being to hit a small rubber puck into the opponents' net

A downhill race with the riders lying on their backs on small sleds

A combination event requiring skills in skiing and ski jumping

Skiers leaping off 70- and 90-meter tracks, landing in a valley below

A timed race on ice of 500–10,000 meters for men and 500–3,000 meters for women

Winter Events Recall

How many events from the Olympic Winter Games can you recall? You may wish to use the cards which you have assembled or test your memory in completing the lists below. Your "target number" is in parentheses.

Events using skis (6)

Events done in pairs (4)

Events needing special equipment (14)

Events taking place on the ice (8)

Team events (5)

Winter Events Recall (cont.)

Events where women compete (12)

Events using skates (5)

Individual events (11)

Events covering long distances (3)

Events with jumping (2)

It is also fun to do this activity as a timed challenge for an individual or a team.

Winter Events Crossword

If you know your winter events, you will be able to solve this crossword in record Olympic Games time!

Across

1. Winter sporting events need _____ .
3. Each sporting contest is known as an _____ .
4. A _____ sled races down an icy track.
6. Two skaters together make up a _____ .
8. This _____ is designed differently for speed and figures.
9. Cross-country skiing is also known as _____ .
11. _____ skating is a graceful sport.
12. There are two or four _____ on a bobsled team.
13. A _____ is a sled that one rides lying on his back.
14. _____ is a form of the slalom.

Down

1. _____ is a sport for people who are not afraid of heights.
2. If a skier falls, his clothes can get _____ .
5. The _____ is a combination of skiing and shooting.
7. _____ is a sport using a puck.
8. A _____ is a type of ski race involving many turns.
10. _____ is a team sport played on ice that was a demonstration sport in seven Olympic Winter Games.

The Marathon

One of the most dramatic single events of every Olympic Games is the marathon. This 26.2 mile (42 km) run, which lasts approximately two and a half hours, is always reserved for the final day of competition. During recent Olympic Games, its finish has been scheduled to coincide with the closing ceremonies. All runners, from the first who wins the gold to the last who struggles into the stadium hours later, are greeted by cheering spectators.

The marathon was never part of the ancient games, but it was introduced at the first modern Olympiad in Athens. Its origin can be traced back to the Greeks. In 490 B.C., a Grecian general named Militades met a force of invading Persians. Although the Greeks were outnumbered ten to one, they staged a furious attack, coming around the Persians' side, and managed to drive them back into the sea. Had the Persians succeeded in their attack, Athens, the capital city of Greece, would have been overrun. All of Greece would have been defeated. This famous Greek victory took place on the plain of Marathon.

As he was eager to get the good news of the victory back to Athens, Militades looked around for his fastest messenger. He chose Pheidippides, a famous long-distance runner. Despite being exhausted from fighting the long battle, Pheidippides ran nonstop over the rough, hilly countryside. When he arrived in Athens, he delivered the good news to the elders of the city, then collapsed and died.

Today's race approximates the distance from the plain of Marathon to Athens. It salutes the memory of the first "gold medal" runner.

The Marathon (cont.)

The marathon is an important part of each Olympic Games. In addition, marathons have come to be run in many cities throughout the world. They draw thousands of participants and are planned and carried out just like the Olympic Games race. Many citizens, young and old, volunteer to help organize the participants, direct traffic, greet spectators, and pass out water to the runners along the way.

1. What training do you think a marathon runner would need?

   _____

   For how long would he/she have to train?

   _____

   For how many hours a day?

   _____

2. Running a marathon is a tremendous challenge. Of the thousands who start, only six are awarded medals (three men and three women). How do you think all the runners-up feel? Is it worth the effort?

   _____

   _____

3. Would you ever consider running a marathon? If so, what preparations would you make? When would you start?

   _____

   _____

4. If a marathon was scheduled for your city, would you like to be a part of it? What would you like to do? (participate, watch it, volunteer to help, etc.)

   _____

   _____

5. Marathon participants are always presented with T-shirts to remember their activity. Design a T-shirt for a marathon to be held in your city. Use the pattern provided on page 135.

6. Get a map of your city and plot the route of a marathon. Remember it is 26.2 miles (42 km), and a city block equals about 100 meters. Have the route pass over some flat land and some hilly land. Pick a good starting point where the runners can assemble. Choose a park or stadium for the finish so the runners can be cheered by a group of spectators.

Event Analogy Challenge

Now that you are familiar with the events of the Olympic and Olympic Winter Games, you are ready for the great analogy challenge. An analogy is used to compare two ideas. To solve it, think how the first set of words is related. Then fill in the blank with a word that relates in the same manner to the word at the end of the sentence.

1. A ball is to field hockey as a p u c k is to ice hockey.

2. Six is to volleyball as __ __ __ __ is to basketball.

3. Paddle is to canoeing as an __ __ __ is to rowing.

4. Racquet is to tennis as a __ __ __ __ __ __ is to table tennis.

5. A foil is to fencing as a __ __ __ __ __ is to boxing.

6. A pommel horse is to a gymnast as a __ __ __ __ __ __ is to a track star.

7. A goal is to soccer as a __ __ __ is to baseball.

8. A ring is to a boxer as a __ __ __ __ is to a curler.

9. A six is to figure skating as a __ __ __ is to gymnastics.

10. An inning is to baseball as a __ __ __ __ __ is to boxing.

11. A broom is to curling as a __ __ __ __ __ is to ice hockey.

12. A net is to team handball as a __ __ __ __ is to basketball.

13. Sit is to a bobsled as __ __ __ is to a luge.

14. A cleat is to a baseball player as a __ __ __ __ __ is to a skater.

15. Shoot is to an arrow as __ __ __ __ __ is to a javelin.

16. Cross-country is to a skier as a __ __ __ __ __ __ __ __ is to a runner.

17. A mat is to a gymnast as a __ __ __ __ __ is to a tennis player.

18. A knockdown is to a boxer as a __ __ __ is to a wrestler.

19. Swimming is to butterfly as __ __ __ __ __ __ __ __ __ __ is to dressage.

20. Alpine is to slalom as __ __ __ __ __ __ is to cross-country.

21. A hand is to water polo as a __ __ __ __ is to soccer.

22. A yacht is to water as a __ __ __ __ is to snow.

23. Pentathlon is to five as __ __ __ __ __ __ __ __ __ is to ten.

24. A scull is to rowing as a __ __ __ __ __ __ __ __ __ is to yachting.

25. A mountain is to a ski jumper as a __ __ __ __ __ __ __ __ is to a diver.

Multi-Contest Events

"Athlon" is a Greek word meaning *contest*. Often Olympic events involve more than one contest. Use these clues to find the events listed in the box. Match them with the correct sports:

bi- = 2   tri- = 3   penta- = 5   hepta- = 7   deca- = 10

1. High jump, high hurdles, shot put, 1,500-meter race, 100-meter race, long jump, discus throw, pole vault, javelin throw, and 400-meter race _____

2. Long jump, discus throw, running, wrestling, and javelin throw _____

3. Cross-country skiing and shooting _____

4. Horseback riding, fencing, pistol shooting, swimming, and running _____

5. 100-meter hurdles, shot put, high jump, long jump, 800-meter race, javelin, and 200-meter race _____

6. Running, swimming, cycling _____

ancient pentathlon	decathlon	heptathlon
modern pentathlon	biathlon	triathlon

7. Create a contest with two to ten events that you like.

Name of contest: _____

Name of events: _____

_____

_____

Where would you hold your contest?

_____

_____

How would you choose the competitors?

_____

_____

_____

A Scoring Challenge

In every Olympic Games, the work of the judges is most important. In some sports, their opinion is the key to a medal. Gymnastics, where an athlete works for a perfect 10, and figure skating, where a 6 is supreme, are scored by decimal points based on set standards for each move. These are added to other points based on the judges' opinions.

Racing events were judged by eye until the 1912 Olympic Games, when an electrical timing device was first introduced. The 1932 Los Angeles Games brought electronic scoring. These devices have improved over the years. Today they are very accurate, measuring the first tip of the swimmer's finger or of the racer's ski on the finish line. The difference between the gold medal winner and a fourth place finisher has been measured in a few hundredths of a second.

To fully enjoy the Olympic Games, it is important to understand the decimal system. Compare the sets of numbers shown below. If you line up two decimals one above the other, matching the decimal points and checking each line from left to right, it is easy to see which is the greater. In the first group of numbers, the second number is smaller and in the second group, the first number is smaller. We can tell by noting the difference in the hundredths place. In the third example, the tenths place gives us the clue that the second number is smaller and the faster time.

1.37
1.34

23.46
23.47

14.50
14.40

On the following page are some actual finish times from swimming and alpine skiing events.

1. Rewrite the numbers from least (the winner) to greatest.

2. Subtract each number from the time just above to find the difference in finishing times.

3. To check your answers, add each of your differences. If your sum equals the target number, you deserve to share the gold.

A Scoring Challenge (cont.)

Freestyle	Breaststroke	Backstroke	Butterfly
Time Difference	Time Difference	Time Difference	Time Difference
51.70	1:04.37	57.28	55.09
51.89	1:03.43	55.49	55.81
49.99	1:03.11	56.34	54.35
51.79	1:04.23	57.69	54.65
50.81	1:04.38	57.49	54.50
51.68	1:04.26	57.22	55.11
Target 1.90	Target 1.27	Target 2.20	Target 1.46

Do the same with these times from women's Alpine ski events.

Slalom	Giant Slalom	Downhill
Time Difference	Time Difference	Time Difference
1:32.31	1:30.49	1:46.68
1:30.87	1:29.95	1:47.71
1:32.24	1:29.25	1:46.16
1:33.24	1:30.44	1:47.50
1:32.20	1:29.13	1:48.58
1:30.54	1:30.40	1:48.48
Target 2.70	Target 1.36	Target 2.42

Challenge!

Which was the closest finish of all the races? _____

In which race did the fourth-place finisher lose a medal by the least amount of time?

_____

Olympic Games Events Sign-Up

Choose an Olympic Games sport that interests you. Sign your name on the line beside it. Use a variety of sources to research and write a report about one or more events in your choosen sport. Use the report form as a guide.

Summer Sports

Archery _____   Athletics (track and field) _____   Badminton _____

Baseball _____   Basketball _____   Boxing _____

Canoeing/kayaking _____   Cycling _____   Diving _____

Equestrian _____   Fencing _____   Field hockey _____

Gymnastics _____   Judo _____   Modern pentathlon _____

Rowing _____   Rhythmic gymnastics _____   Shooting _____

Soccer _____   Softball _____   Swimming _____

Synchronized swimming_____   Table tennis _____   Taekwondo _____

Team handball _____   Tennis _____   Triathlon _____

Volleyball _____   Water polo _____   Weightlifting _____

Wrestling _____   Yachting _____

Winter Sports

Alpine skiing _____   Biathlon _____   Bobsledding _____

Cross-country skiing _____   Curling _____   Figure skating _____

Freestyle skiing _____   Ice hockey _____   Luge _____

Nordic combined skiing _____   Ski jumping _____   Short track skating _____

Snowboarding _____   Speed skating _____

Olympic Games Event Report Form

Name of sport _____

_____
(event)

List the rules for competition in the Olympic Games.

_____

_____

_____

Describe the scoring system for this event.

_____

_____

List the most recent medal winners in this event.

Gold Medal— _____
(Athlete and Country)

Silver Medal— _____
(Athlete and Country)

Bronze Medal— _____
(Athlete and Country)

Mention interesting details about the competition or the life of the winner.

_____

_____

Did the winner(s) of this event win any other events in the same year?

_____

If so, which events? _____

Did the winner(s) of this event ever win the same event or other events in a previous Olympic Games competition? If so, when and what event(s)?

_____

If applicable:

What is the time/distance record for this event? _____

Was a new record set for this event in the last Olympic Games? _____

What country usually wins this event?_____

Olympic Games
Competition

36 USC 220506

What Is a Competitor?

Some people enjoy running for fun and exercise. They have no desire to race. These noncompetitive people perform best when they do not feel pressured. Their goal is personal satisfaction.

Some people enjoy running only when they are racing to see who runs the fastest. These people are competitors. They perform best when testing themselves against their rivals. They enjoy working toward awards, honors, and medals. People who enjoy competition can compete in many areas, not just in sports.

1. Describe how you feel about competition.

   _____

   _____

   _____

2. Tell about a time when you took part in a competition. (It could be anything from soccer to a group project in school.) Did you enjoy the competition? Why or why not? What were the results?

   _____

   _____

3. Name a competition you think you could win. Why do you think you could be successful?

   _____

   _____

4. What are the advantages of being a competitor?

   _____

   _____

5. What are the advantages of being a noncompetitive person?

   _____

   _____

6. What type of person is more likely to become an Olympic Games athlete?

   _____

   _____

Olympic Games Participants

Baron Pierre de Coubertin, founder of the modern Olympic Games, made the following statement which became known as the Olympic Games Creed.

The important thing in the Olympic Games is not to win, but to take part, just as the important thing in life is not the triumph but the struggle; the essential thing is not to have conquered, but to have fought well.

Despite the fact that the Olympic Games stress participation and sportsmanship, everybody always seems to love the winners. As the ancient games grew in popularity, their winners were honored by more than the olive wreath. Various city-states celebrated their heroes' achievements. Some Olympians were offered free meals and lodging for life in the city hall. Others gained prizes equal to an income of 14 years.

Early winners in the modern Olympic Games were not so lucky. James Connolly paid his own way from the United States to the Olympic Games in Athens, Greece, in 1896. He finished first in the triple jump, thus becoming the first American to win an Olympic Games event. Returning home with $.12 in his pocket, he found no one waiting to meet his ship in New York. He spent $.02 on a newspaper to see whether his name was there. It was not there, so he bought himself a $.05 soda to celebrate his return. His final $.05 paid for a ride home on the trolley.

Today, some athletes are richly rewarded by their governments for winning medals, as was the practice in ancient Greece. Still others sign contracts for public appearances or for product endorsements. And, there are those who receive large sums of money for being professional athletes prior to, during, and after the Olympic Games.

Yet, out of the thousands of athletes participating in each Olympic Games, the number of medal winners is few. There are only three medal winners per event, and often the only visible difference between a winner and second place is recorded on an electronic timer. Sometimes athletes are put under tremendous amounts of pressure by their countries to win a medal, and being unable to meet that goal often means disgrace. Most, however, have voiced the same sentiment as the Baron Pierre de Coubertin. He praised the "joy of participation."

Although the names and faces of many gold medalists have become familiar, often it has been the other competitors who have touched the hearts of the world. A few examples follow.

In 1932, Ralph Metcalfe finished behind two of his U.S. teammates to win a bronze medal in the 200-meter race. It was later found that his starting point had accidentally been placed about one meter further back than the rest of the field. His time would have earned him the gold medal. Yet he refused an offer to rerun the race, fearing that the U.S. might not be able to sweep all three medals a second time.

In 1968, John Akhwiri of Tanzania entered the Olympic Games stadium in Mexico City more than one hour after the winner of the grueling 26.2 mile (42 km) marathon. His leg was bloody and bandaged, the result of a severe injury to his knee. He painfully hobbled around the track to the finish line. The crowd cheered Akhwiri as if he were a champion. Although the young Tanzanian was in a lot of pain and knew he would not win a medal, when asked why he did not quit, he replied, "My country did not send me 7,000 miles (11,263 km) to start the race. They sent me 7,000 miles (11,263 km) to finish the race."

Your Personal Goals

What are your personal goals?

_____

_____

_____

What might keep you from fulfilling them?

_____

_____

What can you do to hold onto your goals and finish the race?

_____

_____

Have you ever entered a competition of any kind? If so, what was it? _____

_____

How did you feel? _____

Were you glad you competed?_____

Why or why not? _____

Do you agree with Baron Pierre de Coubertin's statement? _____

Discuss your opinions with your class.

Win or Lose

Imagine that participating in the Olympic Games has been your goal for years. You have competed in the Olympic Games trials, and finally, here you are at the Olympic Games. Maybe you will be an overnight star, or more than likely, you will come out of the competition as a runner-up.

1. Write an entry describing your feelings before your event.

   _____

   _____

   _____

2. Record the details of the competition.

   _____

   _____

   _____

3. The results are in! Congratulations! You are a winner! Place the medal around your neck, and describe your feelings in your journal.

   _____

   _____

   _____

4. Suppose you did not win a medal in the Olympic Games. Describe your feelings.

   _____

   _____

   _____

5. What are your future plans?

   _____

   _____

   _____

For Amateurs Only

In the 1912 Olympic Games, Jim Thorpe, a Native American from Oklahoma, won the pentathlon and the decathlon. To win the pentathlon, he had to make the best combined score in five track and field events. The decathlon consisted of ten events. Thorpe was widely hailed in 1912 as the world's greatest all-around athlete. All this changed in 1913 when it was discovered that Thorpe had once received $15 a week to play minor league baseball, then a non-Olympic Games sport. His awards were sent back to the Olympic Games officials who offered them to the second place winners of the pentathlon and decathlon. Both second place winners refused to accept Thorpe's gold medals.

Despite the controversy, Jim Thorpe was voted by sportswriters in 1950 as the greatest American athlete of the 20th century. In 1973, 20 years after the champion's death, his amateur status was reinstated by the American Athletic Union. Jim Thorpe is the most famous example of the Olympic Games Committee's enforcement of the discontinued rule allowing only amateur athletes as competitors.

But what was an amateur? Many found the rules confusing. Babe Didrikson, the star of the 1932 Olympic Games, was barred from further Olympic Games competition when her picture appeared in an automobile advertisement. She claimed she had received no payment, but it did not help her cause when a new red Dodge coupe showed up in her driveway. Another victim of the regulations was the great runner from Finland, Paavo Nurmi. Winner of six gold medals in 1920, 1924, and 1928, he was forbidden to compete in the 1932 Games as he had accepted money for public appearances.

In 1960, the International Olympic Games Committee (IOC) defined an amateur as *one who participates and always has participated solely for pleasure . . . and to whom participation in sport is nothing more than recreation without material gain of any kind, direct or indirect.* Clauses were added to ban athletes from many other practices, among them advertising, endorsing products, or receiving help in training from businesses or governments.

Enforcing the amateur rule against individual athletes proved easier than against entire teams or nations. The winning Japanese women's volleyball team was composed of young women kept segregated to endure vigorous, sometimes cruel, training for most of the year. For years, Soviet and East European athletes were supported and trained by their governments. Even though these teams and athletes were not paid as professionals, they certainly could not be called amateur. That contributed to the joy of victory when the strictly amateur U.S. hockey teams of 1960 and 1980 were able to win gold medals against such competitors.

In 1971, the IOC dropped the word "amateur" and attempted instead to define positive rules of eligibility. This led to even more confusion. During recent years it has been left up to each individual sport's federation to make its own rules for Olympic Games competition.

Professional athletes now participate in Olympic competition in basketball, ice hockey, soccer, tennis, beach volleyball, and cycling, but may not receive money or accept endorsements during a set period of time prior to, or during, the Olympic Games and Olympic Winter Games, in accordance with the IOC charter's rules and by-laws.

For Amateurs Only (cont.)

Although defeated in 1972 and 1988, the U.S. has won more gold medals in men's basketball than has any other country. In 1992, the U.S. men's basketball team, nicknamed the "Dream Team," was dominated by well-known professional players.

In 1988, tennis became an official Olympic Games sport, and many well-known stars took to the court in hopes of Olympic gold. Professionals who took part included Sweden's Stefan Edberg, Germany's Steffi Graf, and the U.S.A.'s Chris Evert, Pam Shriver, and Zina Garrison.

A major breakthrough for figure skaters came in 1994 when those who had turned professional were again given Olympic Games eligibility. This ruling saw stars such as Brian Boitano and Katerina Witt once again on Olympic Games ice. Some returned because they wanted to compete with the very best in the world and perhaps gain another medal. Others, realizing there were young talented athletes ready for the gold, simply wanted to renew the wonderful Olympic Games experience. Undoubtedly, there will continue to be changes in the future.

There are mixed feelings about allowing professional athletes and teams to compete in the Olympic Games. If the Olympic Games are to reflect the best talent in the world, some say, then let them come. However, there are only so many spots on each country's team. If these spots are filled with professionals, up-and-coming young athletes will miss the chance to display their talents and participate in the Olympic Games. Many of today's professional athletes might have missed their opportunity for stardom had they not first shared in Olympic Games glory.

Choose some members of your class who would be interested in debating the pros and cons of amateur competition. Prepare and stage a debate on the subject. Work with a group to compile a list of well-known athletes whose careers were launched by their participation in an Olympic Games.

No Drugs Allowed

Testing athletes for drug use became official at the 1968 Olympic Games in Mexico City. Since then, the International Olympic Games Committee has been strict in enforcing its very precise drug abuse rules.

The greatest drug controversy has been centered around the use of steroids. Properly called anabolic-androgenic steroids (AAS), many young people foolishly believe that these drugs can improve athletic performance. In reality, the irreparable harm that these drugs cause easily outnumbers any possible benefits the user could hope to attain. The American Sports Education Institute found that, in addition to physical damage, psychological side effects include "wide mood swings ranging from periods of violent, even homicidal, episodes known as 'roid rages,' to depression, paranoid jealousy, extreme irritability, delusions, and impaired judgment."

The use of AAS for muscle building or improving athletic performance has been deplored by many national organizations with knowledge of the damage steroids can cause. Among those denouncing the use of steroids are the American Medical Association, the U.S. Olympic Committee, the International Olympic Committee, the National Collegiate Athletic Association, and the National Football League.

By the 1976 Olympic Games in Montreal, drug testing was in force. Tests detected users among some weight lifters, and medals had to be returned. One female discus thrower from Poland also tested positive. In 1988, sprinter Ben Johnson of Canada edged out Carl Lewis of the United States in a close finish of the 100-meter dash. His gold medal was later taken away and awarded to Lewis when tests showed the presence of steroids in Johnson's body. Steroids and other debilitating drugs have no place in Olympic Games competition.

In fact, the International Olympic Games Committee takes drug usage so seriously that horses competing in Olympic Games Equestrian events may not be given performance-enhancing drugs.

No Drugs Allowed (cont.)

There is no disagreement, however, about the risks of taking steroids. Liver problems, including liver cancer, may result. Changes in digestive functions can lead to heart disease and high blood pressure. The reproductive system can be affected. Bone development can be slowed, causing joint problems and stunted growth. However, some young athletes think only of immediate success. Unfortunately, some of their coaches and even some of their doctors also view the importance of excelling in a sport as more important than the health of the individual.

The spirit of competition and the goals of the Olympic Games are never considered.

Think about some of the immediate effects of steroids on the body.

Which are good?   **Which are bad?**

_____   _____
_____   _____
_____   _____
_____   _____

What are the long-range effects of steroids on the body?

Which are good?   **Which are bad?**

_____   _____
_____   _____
_____   _____
_____   _____

If an athlete was found to have taken steroids before competition, what would happen?

_____

If he/she tested positive for steroids after competition, what would happen?

_____

How might steroids affect the character of an athlete?

_____

How many other persons might his/her cheating affect?

_____

Working with your friends, plan a skit about an athlete considering the use of steroids in order to excel in a sport. Present your skit to your classmates.

Olympians Don't Quit

Did you ever want to give up because something happened that made your goal harder to achieve? It has happened to Olympians, too.

Dutch athlete Fanny Blankers-Koen, age 22, was looking forward to the 1940 Olympic Games, sure she would win the gold as a sprinter. But World War II came along, and both the 1940 and the 1944 Olympic Games were canceled. She continued training, gave birth to a son and a daughter, and looked forward to the 1948 games. By that time Fanny was 30, much older than the other sprinters. She won the 100-meter dash and the 80-meter hurdles, only to be mobbed by reporters who would not let her rest for her remaining events. Yet she went on to win the 200-meter race and was a member of the winning 4 x 100-meter relay. Fanny was the first woman ever to have won four track and field gold medals in the same Olympiad.

In 1938, Hungarian army sergeant Karoly Takacs was a member of his national pistol shooting team and expected to win in the 1940 Olympic Games, but a tragic accident happened. While he was on maneuvers, a hand grenade exploded, leaving Karoly without his right hand, his shooting hand. His hopes for gold dashed, Takacs was allowed to remain in the army, despite his disability. He was severely depressed, but he began training again with a pistol, this time using his left hand. At the 1948 Olympic Games, Captain Takacs stood on the winner's platform wearing his gold medal for pistol shooting. He won it with his left hand, the hand he had never used for shooting prior to the accident ten years earlier.

Ray Ewry of Lafayette, Indiana, was paralyzed as a child and spent much of his childhood in a wheelchair. Doctors believed that he would never walk again. He devoted hours to exercise and not only walked, but developed great strength in his legs. He won the three jumping events at Paris in 1900 at the age of 26, repeated his performance at St. Louis in 1904, and once again swept the jumping events at the 1908 Olympic Games in London.

When Wilma Rudolph was four, she caught scarlet fever and pneumonia. It was thought she would never walk again. Yet, her mother drove her long distances to therapy, and her brothers and sisters spent many hours massaging her useless legs. By age six, she was walking in special shoes. But Wilma did not stop there. In high school, she starred in basketball. Switching to track, she made the Olympic Games team in 1956 and won two bronze medals. In 1960, she returned from the Games with three gold medals. She was a winner personally, too, being one of the most popular athletes of all time.

Like most boys growing up in Flint, Michigan, trying out for Little League was an important part of life for young Jim Abbott. The fact that he did not have a right hand made no difference. At an early age he had learned to pitch and bat lefthanded. When catching a ball in the field, he wore the glove on his left hand, quickly switching it to his right as he threw the runners out. At the University of Michigan, Jim pitched his way to many honors, including the Big Ten Player of the Year. As a member of the 1988 Olympic Games team, he made two appearances on the mound. In the final game against Japan, he pitched a complete game to clinch the gold medal for the USA. He was no longer thought of as a player with one hand. Although Jim had reached his lifetime goal of earning an Olympic Games gold medal, he continued his athletic career by pitching in professional Major League Baseball.

Olympians Don't Quit (cont.)

Directions: In the following word search you will find words related to the lives of several Olympians who never gave up. The words are hidden horizontally, vertically, diagonally, forward, and backward. Circle the words and place them in the paragraphs on the following page to retell the stories of these great athletes.

```
T  H  R  E  E  B  I  G  T  E  N  P  V  A
D  L  O  G  U  J  A  P  A  N  L  O  I  V
K  W  I  L  M  A  T  I  Y  T  R  A  C  K
G  H  O  W  A  R  O  S  R  Y  S  N  T  W
L  E  C  A  B  B  O  T  T  R  M  P  O  S
F  E  W  P  Y  E  H  O  D  W  R  B  R  A
N  L  F  Y  A  G  S  L  C  E  S  A  Y  I
A  C  E  T  I  F  A  N  N  Y  W  S  C  N
G  H  O  R  H  F  I  E  L  D  N  K  E  T
I  A  L  O  D  A  E  M  L  P  G  E  Z  L
H  I  T  P  G  T  N  R  F  S  O  T  N  O
C  R  A  S  I  P  O  D  I  U  M  B  O  U
I  V  K  L  A  W  J  R  E  M  D  A  R  I
M  Z  A  E  H  A  A  B  B  D  T  L  B  S
F  N  C  G  J  P  N  O  D  N  O  L  B  C
W  O  S  L  K  J  D  T  H  I  R  T  Y  A
```

Cross off the words as you find them: gold, Abbott, right, lefthanded, Michigan, Wilma, Big Ten, Japan, track, victory, wheelchair, London, thirty, bronze, Saint Louis, basketball, field, pistol, shoot, podium, walk, Ewry, Takacs, world war, Paris, three, leg, Fanny

Olympians Don't Quit (cont.)

Directions: Using the words found in the preceding word search, fill in the blanks below and retell the stories of these great athletes.

_____ pitcher Jim _____ led his team at the

University of _____ and was named outstanding player in

the _____ . He pitched his USA team to _____ over _____

in the 1988 Games.

_____ Rudolph showed her family and friends that indeed she would _____ again.

She starred in high school _____ and went out for _____.

She won two Olympic _____ medals in 1956 and returned to

win _____ gold medals in 1960.

Roy _____ left his _____ and exercised to develop

great _____ strength. He became an outstanding jumper and swept those events

in the _____ Games of 1900 and repeated his performance in the

following Olympic Games at _____ and

_____.

_____Blankers-Koen missed two Olympic Games because of _____

_____. In 1948, at age _____, she became the first woman to win four _____

and _____ events.

In 1938, Karoly _____ looked forward to winning the gold medal

in _____ shooting. In a tragic accident, he lost his _____ hand.

Rather than give up his sport, he taught himself to _____ with his other hand,

and in the 1948 Olympic Games he stood on the _____

with a _____ medal around his neck.

Famous Olympians

If the names of famous Olympians were placed end to end, they could probably circle the globe many times. Here is an introduction to a few who earned the gold. Perhaps you will read to find out more about them. It is hoped you will continue your search to become acquainted with still other equally famous Olympic Games stars.

U.S. Olympic Games Stars

In Athletics (track and field) events, the name of Jesse Owens, the sharecropper's son from Alabama, always tops the list of favorite Olympians. His four gold medals won at the 1936 Berlin Olympic Games discredited Hitler's notion of German superiority over other races.

In 1984, another track sensation by the name of Carl Lewis matched Jesse Owens' performance of 28 years before and went on to excel in the 1988, 1992, and 1996 Games.

Babe Didrikson was the track star of the 1932 Olympic Games, capturing a gold medal for the U.S. in the javelin throw and another in the 800-meter hurdles. She went on to become a golf star and is still considered one of the most versatile female athletes.

The decathlon winner usually holds the honor of being considered the world's best athlete. In 1948, Bob Mathias became the youngest man to earn the gold. Four years later he won again at the age of 21. Other honored decathlon winners include Rafer Johnson (1960), Bill Toomey (1968), Bruce Jenner (1976), and Dan O'Brien (1996).

Swimming and diving have seen their champions, too. After winning five gold medals in swimming in 1924 and 1928, Johnny Weissmuller went on to play the original Tarzan. Patricia McCormick practiced over 100 dives a day to achieve her goal. She swept the diving events for the United States in both the 1956 and 1960 Olympic Games. Her daughter also went on to medal in diving in the 1984 and 1988 Olympic Games.

Greg Louganis, protégé of the 1948 Olympic Games diving star Dr. Sammy Lee, began his Olympic diving carreer in 1976, winning the silver medal on platform at the age of 16. Louganis won gold medals in the 1984 and 1988 Games. After winning two bronze medals in 1968, Mark Spitz came back to earn seven gold medals in swimming events in the l972 Olympic Games in Munich.

Eddie Eagan won a gold medal in boxing in 1920 and another in four-man bobsledding in 1932. He is the only athlete to have won a gold medal in both the Olympic Games and the Olympic Winter Games.

In 1980, speed skater Eric Heiden became the first to win five individual gold medals in his sport. Speed skater Bonnie Blair won five gold medals between 1988 and 1994.

The sport of figure skating has brought the gold to the U.S. quite often. Winners include Tenley Albright (1956), Carol Heiss (1960), Peggy Fleming (1968), Dorothy Hamill (1976), Kristy Yamaguchi (1992), and Tara Lipinski (1998). Dick Button was a two-time gold medal winner for the men (1948 and 1952) and continued to participate in many Olympic Games as a television commentator on his sport. Hayes Alan Jenkins won a skating gold in 1956, and his brother David took it in 1960. Other men's winners include Scott Hamilton (1984) and Brian Boitano (1988).

Famous Olympians (cont.)

Some of the most familiar names among past U.S. Olympians are found in the boxing world. Floyd Patterson won the gold for the United States in the 1952 Games and later became the heavyweight champion of the world. George Foreman won the gold in the super heavyweight division in 1968. As a professional, he defeated the 1964 winner, Joe Frazier. Later he lost to the gold medal winner of the 1960 Games, Cassius Clay, known to boxing fans as Muhammad Ali.

Other famous U.S. Olympians include:

Andrea Mead Lawrence of Vermont who was the first U.S. woman to win two medals in Alpine skiing.

Harrison "Bones" Dillard who was considered one of the greatest hurdlers of all times. He won four gold medals for the U.S. in 1948 and 1952.

Al Oerter who threw the discus to win the gold in four Olympic Games (1956–1968).

Parry O'Brian who threw the shot put in four Olympic Games (1952–1964) for two gold medals and a silver medal.

Famous Olympians (cont.)

Foreign Stars

Leonidas of Rhodes, perhaps the greatest runner of all time, won the 200- meter, 400- meter, and hoplite in four Olympic Games from 164 B.C. to 152 B.C.

Paavo Nurmi, known as the "flying Finn," first competed in 1920. He won seven gold and three silver medals for Finland over three Olympic Games. He was known for his explosive starts and habit of boasting ahead of time about his winning performances.

Daley Thompson of Great Britain became the pride of his country by winning the decathlon in 1980 and 1984.

Dawn Fraser, Australia's popular freestyle swimmer, competed in three successive Olympic Games (1956, 1960, and 1964). She earned one silver and five gold medals.

Sonja Henie of Norway was only 11 years old when she appeared in her first Olympic Games in 1924. She did not win that year, but she later won three gold medals in figure skating (1928, 1932, and 1936). After her figure skating career she became a popular movie star.

In 1956, Anton (Tony) Sailer became the hero of Austria as the first skier to sweep gold medals in all three Alpine events.

In 1968, Jean Claude Killy of France succeeded in repeating Sailer's feat. In 1992, he was once again in the spotlight as he secured and organized the Games for Albertville, France. These Games took place in the Alpine mountains only a few miles from where Killy had grown up and first learned to ski.

The West Germans were hoping for the same three Alpine medals in 1976 from their skiing sensation, Rosi Mittermaier. She won the first two races but lost the Giant Slalom by only .12 of a second.

The beginning of the gymnastic craze is often credited to 17-year-old Olga Korbut of the Soviet Union, but she did not win a gold medal in individual event competition. Her aggressive and daring style amazed the fans at the 1972 Games. Four years later, Nadia Comaneci of Romania collected seven perfect tens, the highest score in gymnastics. Nadia won three gold medals in Montreal in 1976 and two in Moscow in 1980.

The continent of Africa has been the home of many brilliant runners. Abebe Bikila, used to running barefoot in his native Ethiopia, saw no reason to put on shoes as he ran the marathon in the 1960 Olympic Games. After winning the gold medal in two hours and 15 minutes, he still had enough energy to take a victory lap around the stadium. In 1964, he again won the marathon, this time wearing shoes. He is the only man in Olympic Games history to win two consecutive marathons.

Runner Kipchoge Keino of Kenya won two gold and two silver medals over two Olympic Games (1968 and 1972). He wore a cap when he raced and delighted in tossing it to the crowd as he completed his final lap.

Famous Olympians (cont.)

How well do you remember the Olympic Games stars? Match each star below with his/her description in the opposite column. Use a ruler to draw a straight line from one to the other.

Sammy Lee   •   • Popular woman diver

Abebe Bikila   •   • Norway's skating queen

Dawn Fraser   •   • Barefoot marathon winner

Jesse Owen   •   • Became heavyweight champ of the world

Olga Korbut   •   • Almost swept the Alpine for her country

Eric Heiden   •   • Winning Australian swimmer

Cassius Clay   •   • Track star, Berlin Games

Eddie Eagan   •   • Won seven gold medals in swimming

Mark Spitz   •   • Winter and summer medalist

Rosi Mittermaier   •   • Sparked interest in gymnastics

Babe Didrikson   •   • Youngest decathlon winner

Patricia McCormick   •   • Won diving gold and coached another winner

Daley Thompson   •   • Swept Alpine events

Sonja Henie   •   • U.S. figure skating champ

Jean Claude Killy   •   • Won five golds in speed skating

Bob Mathias   •   • Two time decathlon winner for Great Britain

Dick Button   •   • Great all-around female athlete

(boxes scattered in the middle column: I, 7, 3, E, 8, S, 12, 13, E, H, S, 4, T, H, 9, I, 16, 17, 2, I, S, R, 14, T, 15, P, 5, 6, T, T, 1, U, 10, S, 11)

As you draw each straight line, you will notice that it passes through one square with a **number** in it and through one square with a **letter.** Below you will find a row of numbered boxes. **Place the letters in the boxes with their matching numbers.** (One is already done for you.) If you have matched all the stars correctly, you will find the answer to this riddle.

What did the ancient Olympian say when he lost his olive wreath?

1	2	3	4	5	6	7	8	9	10	11	12	13	14	15	16	17	!
T																	

Olympic Star Profile Sign-Up

Below are former Olympians with whom you may be familiar. Select one of these athletes and sign your name on the line beside your choice. Read further about this athlete and use the profile sheet to report on your findings.

Jim Abbott_____	Michael Jordan _____
John Stephen Akhwiri_____	Jackie Joyner-Kersee_____
Tenley Albright_____	Kipchoge Keino _____
Abebe Bikila_____	Nancy Kerrigan_____
Matt Biondi_____	Jean Claude Killy _____
Bonnie Blair _____	Olga Korbut_____
Fanny Blankers-Koen _____	Andrea Mead Lawrence _____
Brian Boitano _____	Sammy Lee_____
Dick Button_____	Leonidas of Rhodes _____
Cassius Clay _____	Carl Lewis_____
Nadia Comaneci _____	Greg Louganis_____
James Connolly_____	Bob Mathias _____
Babe Didrikson _____	Patricia McCormick _____
Eddie Eagan _____	Ralph Metcalfe _____
Janet Evans _____	Rosi Mittermaier_____
Ray Ewry _____	Shannon Miller _____
Peggy Fleming _____	Milo of Croton _____
George Foreman _____	Paavo Nurmi_____
Dawn Fraser _____	Dan O'Brien _____
Joe Frazier_____	Parry O'Brien _____
Florence Griffith-Joyner _____	Al Oerter_____
Dorothy Hamill_____	Jesse Owens _____
Eric Heiden _____	Floyd Patterson _____
Carol Heiss _____	Mary Lou Retton_____
Sonja Henie_____	Daley Thompson_____
Dan Jansen _____	Jim Thorpe _____
Alan Hayes Jenkins_____	Bill Toomey _____
David Jenkins _____	Johnny Weissmuller _____
Bruce Jenner _____	Katerina Witt_____
Rafer Johnson _____	Kristy Yamaguchi _____

Olympic Star Profile Report Form

Choose one of your favorite Olympic Games stars to research and profile.

Star's Name: _____

Country: _____

Olympic Games Year(s): _____

Event(s) Won: _____

Record(s) Set: _____

Interesting facts about this athlete: _____

_____

_____

_____

_____

_____

_____

_____

_____

_____

_____

Don't Forget to Write

Choose an athlete from one of the Olympic Games. Pretend you are that athlete and write a postcard home to your family. Tell your family about the host city and about some of the athletes you have met. Be sure you have the athlete placed at the right Olympic Games. Include some details about your competition. Then cut your postcard out, turn it over, and draw a picture so everyone back home can share your fun.

This Is My Country

Put yourself in the shoes of a competitor from a past Olympic Games. As you pretend to be that athlete, answer the following questions about "your" country to share with your fellow Olympians.

My country is _____.

Here is its flag.

How large is your country?_____

Where is it located? _____

What is the land like (flat and/or mountainous)? _____

What is its population (number of people)?_____

What is the capital city? _____

What other large cities are in your country? _____

_____

How do the people earn a living?_____

_____

_____

What are some of your country's products that are shipped around the world? _____

_____

Tell a little about the history of your country. _____

_____

_____

_____

Who are some of your country's famous people (past or present)?_____

_____

_____

_____

This Is My Country (cont.)

You have made some new friends at the Olympic Games. Suppose you invited them to visit you when you returned home.

What would be a good month to come?_____

What would the weather be like then? _____

_____

What kind of clothes should they pack?_____

_____

How do the people in your country dress?_____

_____

_____

Do they have any traditional dress that they wear for holidays? If so, describe it. _____

_____

Tell about some of the holidays your visitors might enjoy. _____

_____

_____

What favorite foods would you want to serve your visitors?_____

_____

_____

What are some of the interesting sights you would want to show them? _____

_____

_____

What would you do with your friends to have fun?_____

_____

_____

If they wanted to shop for souvenirs to remember their visit, what would you suggest they buy?

_____

_____

How Does It "Suit" You?

Besides holding trials to choose the best athletes for the Olympic Games team, each Olympic Games Committee must make many other plans.

One of these is choosing the design for the outfits the athletes will wear.

A somewhat formal outfit is usually worn at the opening ceremonies. Its colors and design are chosen to represent the spirit of the country.

Each athlete also has an outfit to wear for competition. These differ according to the sport.

Informal sweats and a warm-up jacket are also part of each athlete's wardrobe. These are worn while waiting for competition and while relaxing around the Olympic Games village.

Think of an original design for informal clothing for your country's athletes to wear to the next Olympic Games. Place your designs on the models below.

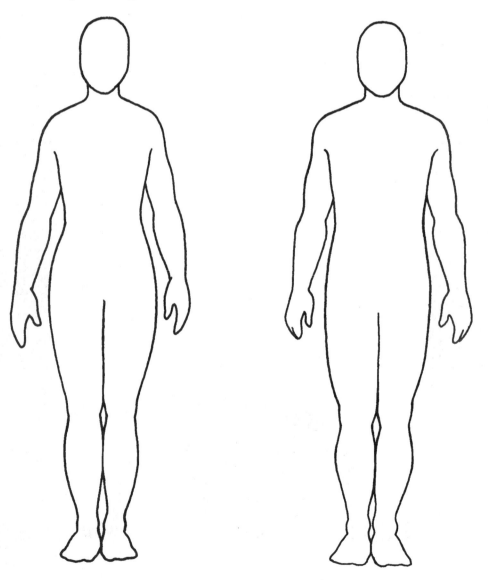

The Olympic Games and You

36 USC 220506

An Olympic Games ABC Book

Think back over what you have learned about the Olympic Games. Choose one significant word relating to the Olympic Games, beginning with each letter of the alphabet. Write your words on the lines below. (**Hint:** When you run into a tough letter like Q, do not forget the names of some competing countries or their athletes.)

A _____   N _____

B _____   O _____

C _____   P _____

D _____   Q _____

E _____   R _____

F _____   S _____

G _____   T _____

H _____   U _____

I _____   V _____

J _____   W _____

K _____   X _____

L _____   Y _____

M _____   Z _____

- When you have completed your list, follow the directions below to turn it into an ABC book.

- Choose a symbol that is representative of the Olympic Games (the logo of the discus thrower, the torch, etc.).

- Draw it on a piece of railroad board. This is your front cover.

- Color or paint it decoratively.

- Then cut it out around the shape.

- Trace and cut out another piece of railroad board for the back cover.

- Carefully cut out 26 sheets of paper in the same shape.

- On each sheet, write a letter of the alphabet and the word you have chosen for that letter.

- Write a definition for each word.

- Assemble your book and share it with your classmates.

Road to the Olympic Games

Road to the Olympic Games is a board game for two to six players. It provides students the opportunity to apply what they have learned about the Olympic Games.

Preparation

- Reproduce, construct, color, mount, and possibly laminate the game board (pages 102–105). Your students will enjoy helping.
- Reproduce and cut apart the questions (pages 92–101). They are printed so they may be easily copied with the answers on the reverse side. Additional question cards may be prepared to reflect your class's interests and knowledge.
- Make a copy of the rules by which to play.
- Supply tokens.

How to Play

You are a young athlete. To make it to the Olympic Games you need to start early. Will you win your school events? Can you make it to your country's Olympic Games trials? Will you make the Olympic Games team?

The object of this game is to be the first player to cross the finish line and win the Olympic Games gold medal. There are three main pathways you must travel: *School Events, Olympic Games Trials*, and, finally, the *Olympic Games*. In order to move around these tracks, you must answer questions about the Olympic Games. As you make your way to the finish line, watch out. There are setbacks that will slow your progress. Yet, in some spaces you will find a bonus to help you on your way.

Shuffle the question cards and place them on the board. Decide who will go first. That player (athlete) takes the top card from the stack. The player (athlete) on his/her left reads the question. If the first player answers the question correctly, he/she moves down the pathway according to the number of spaces that appears on the card. The next player then takes a card and repeats the process. If a player cannot answer a question, he/she forfeits a turn. The winner is the first to cross the finish line.

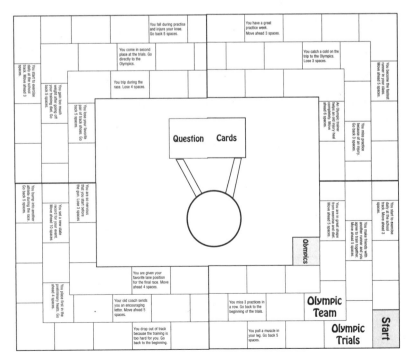

Road to the Olympic Games (cont.)

Directions: Cut apart the cards, match them to the answers on page 93, and then glue or tape them back-to-back.

1. In what country did the Olympic Games begin?	2. How many years are there between Olympic Winter Games?	3. Who was excluded from the ancient Olympic Games?
4. What is the prize for first place at the Olympic Games?	5. What city was the site of the ancient Olympic Games?	6. Who was Baron de Coubertin?
7. What prize was given for winning at the ancient Olympic Games?	8. Of what is the third place medal made?	9. Name the years of the next three Summer Olympic Games.
10. Name the years of the next three Winter Olympic Games.	11. How many days did the ancient Olympic Games take?	12. What race started the ancient Olympic Games?
13. What was the roughest sport of the ancient Olympic Games?	14. What was a *stade*?	15. Who was honored at the ancient Olympic Games?
16. What did ancient Olympic judges use to enforce the rules?	17. In what year did the modern Olympic Games begin?	18. Name a hero of the ancient Olympic Games.
19. In what year did the ancient Olympic Games begin?	20. Who was Hera?	21. When were the first Winter Olympic Games?
22. The ancient pancratium consisted of a combination of what modern sports?	23. Name three of the sports of the ancient pentathlon.	24. What was the first sport women played in the Olympic Games?

Road to the Olympic Games (cont.)

Directions: Cut apart the cards, match them to the questions on page 92, and then glue or tape them back-to-back.

1. Greece Move ahead 1 space.	2. four Move ahead 1 space.	3. women Move ahead 1 space.
4. gold medal Move ahead 1 space.	5. Olympia Move ahead 2 spaces.	6. founder of modern Olympic Games Move ahead 2 spaces.
7. olive wreath Move ahead 2 spaces.	8. bronze Move ahead 2 spaces.	9. 2000, 2004, and 2008 Move ahead 3 spaces.
10. 2002, 2006, and 2010 Move ahead 3 spaces.	11. five Move ahead 3 spaces.	12. chariot race Move ahead 3 spaces.
13. chariot race Move ahead 4 spaces.	14. length of stadium (about 200 meters) Move ahead 4 spaces.	15. Greek gods, especially Zeus Move ahead 4 spaces.
16. used rods Move ahead 4 spaces.	17. 1896 Move ahead 5 spaces.	18. Milo of Croton, Leonidis of Rhodes Move ahead 5 spaces.
19. 776 B.C. Move ahead 5 spaces.	20. wife of Zeus Move ahead 5 spaces.	21. 1924 Move ahead 6 spaces.
22. boxing, wrestling, and judo Move ahead 6 spaces.	23. long jump, javelin, footrace, discus, and wrestling Move ahead 6 spaces.	24. lawn tennis Move ahead 6 spaces.

Road to the Olympic Games (cont.)

Directions: Cut apart the cards, match them to the answers on page 95, and then glue or tape them back-to-back.

1. What is used to light the Olympic flame?	2. How do the athletes promise to observe good sportsmanship?	3. When is the Olympic flame lit?
4. What are the six colors of the Olympic flag?	5. Who carries the flag of each country into the stadium?	6. How was the torch used in the ancient Olympic Games?
7. What did the five rings stand for in ancient Greece?	8. What do the five rings represent today?	9. Name the five continents the rings represent.
10. Where were the rings displayed in ancient Greece?	11. Name one of the words in the Olympic motto.	12. Why are doves sometimes released at the Games?
13. Which country's athletes are the first to enter the opening ceremonies?	14. In what order do the athletes enter for opening ceremonies?	15. Who leads the athletes in reciting the Olympic oath?
16. In the ancient Games, who lit the flame?	17. At which of the modern Olympic Games was the flame first lit?	18. Who first entered the arena during the ancient Games?
19. What did the ancient judges wear?	20. What does the marathon commemorate?	21. What did the herald do at ancient Games?
22. At what Olympic Games was the flag first flown?	23. In what country was the Olympic flag first displayed?	24. What is the motto of the Olympic Games?

Road to the Olympic Games (cont.)

Directions: Cut apart the cards, match them to the questions on page 94, and then glue or tape them back-to-back.

1. Olympic torch Move ahead 2 spaces.	2. They take the Olympic oath. Move ahead 1 space.	3. at the opening ceremonies Move ahead 1 space.
4. red, blue, green, yellow, black, white Move ahead 2 spaces.	5. a member of the team usually chosen by teammates Move ahead 2 spaces.	6. to light the fire for the sacrifice Move ahead 2 spaces.
7. represented the years between Olympic Games Move ahead 3 spaces.	8. the participating continents Move ahead 2 spaces.	9. Europe, Africa, Asia, Australia, North and South America Move ahead 2 spaces.
10. They were found on an ancient Greek altar. Move ahead 3 spaces.	11. Citius, Altius, Fortius, (Swifter, Higher, Stronger) Move ahead 3 spaces.	12. They symbolize peace. Move ahead 3 spaces.
13. Greek team Move ahead 4 spaces.	14. alphabetical order Move ahead 4 spaces.	15. usually one of the athletes from the host country Move ahead 4 spaces.
16. winner of the footrace Move ahead 5 spaces.	17. 1896, Athens Move ahead 5 spaces.	18. judges Move ahead 4 spaces.
19. purple robes Move ahead 6 spaces.	20. the Greek battle at Marathon Move ahead 5 spaces.	21. announced athlete's name, father, city Move ahead 5 spaces.
22. 1920, Antwerp Move ahead 6 spaces.	23. Paris, France Move ahead 6 spaces.	24. Citus, Altius, Fortius, (Swifter, Higher, Stronger) Move ahead 6 spaces.

Road to the Olympic Games (cont.)

Directions: Cut apart the cards, match them to the answers on page 97, and then glue or tape them back-to-back.

1. What city hosted the first modern Olympic Games?	2. What U.S. city has hosted two Olympic Games?	3. What was the last city to host the Olympic Games?
4. What was the last year the Olympic Games were in the U.S.?	5. Name a country that has hosted both Summer and Olympic Winter Games.	6. Where were the Olympic Games in 1984?
7. What animal was chosen as the first Olympic mascot?	8. What must a city have to host Olympic Winter Games?	9. Who was Sam the Eagle?
10. What U.S. city was first to host the Olympic Games?	11. What two U.S. states were sites of Winter Olympic Games?	12. What city in Japan hosted an Olympic Games?
13. Most Olympic Games have been held on what continent?	14. What country held Olympic Winter Games at Calgary?	15. What country held the first Olympic Winter Games?
16. Name a country that hosted the Olympic Games twice in one year.	17. Why did mostly U.S. athletes attend the St. Louis Olympic Games?	18. Where is Lake Placid?
19. Name the Olympic Games that had a tiger for a mascot.	20. Name a year when no Olympic Games took place.	21. Name a capital city in North America that was an Olympic Games site.
22. Name the Olympic Winter Games that had twins for mascots.	23. Name five sites of Olympic competion in the U.S.	24. What country has hosted the most Olympic Games?

Road to the Olympic Games (cont.)

Directions: Cut apart the cards, match them to the questions on page 96, and then glue or tape them back-to-back.

1. Athens Move ahead 2 spaces.	2. Los Angeles, CA Move ahead 1 space.	3. Answers will vary. Move ahead 1 space.
4. 1996 Move ahead 1 space. (answers will vary)	5. France, U.S., Japan, Canada, Italy Move ahead 2 spaces.	6. Los Angeles, CA Move ahead 2 spaces.
7. a dog (dachshund) Move ahead 2 spaces.	8. snow Move ahead 2 spaces.	9. mascot, Los Angeles, CA, 1984 Move ahead 3 spaces.
10. St. Louis Move ahead 3 spaces.	11. CA, NY Move ahead 3 spaces.	12. Tokyo or Nagano Move ahead 3 spaces.
13. Europe Move ahead 4 spaces.	14. Canada Move ahead 4 spaces.	15. France Move ahead 4 spaces.
16. USA, France Move ahead 4 spaces.	17. travel problem for athletes Move ahead 5 spaces.	18. New York, USA Move ahead 5 spaces.
19. Seoul, Korea Move ahead 5 spaces.	20. 1916, 1940, and 1944 Move ahead 5 spaces.	21. Mexico City Move ahead 6 spaces.
22. Calgary Move ahead 6 spaces.	23. Los Angeles, St. Louis, Atlanta, Squaw Valley, and Lake Placid Move ahead 6 spaces.	24. USA (seven) Move ahead 6 spaces.

Road to the Olympic Games (cont.)

Directions: Cut apart the cards, match them to the answers on page 99, and then glue or tape them back-to-back.

1. What is the longest race in the Olympic Games?	2. How many miles in a marathon?	3. Which Olympic Games has more events, summer or winter?
4. How many events are there in a pentathlon?	5. Name a team game in the Olympic Winter Games.	6. In what event is a pole used?
7. In what sport do athletes perform a synchronized routine?	8. Name one Alpine skiing event.	9. What equipment is used in cross country?
10. How many events in a decathlon?	11. Name two events in figure skating.	12. Name the two sports in the biathlon.
13. Name two winter sports where men and women are paired.	14. In what position do luge riders race?	15. What is a luge?
16. Name two objects that a track and field athlete throws.	17. Name an event that both men and women gymnasts perform.	18. In what sport are a hoop and ball used?
19. Name a sport where 10 is a perfect score.	20. How does a gymnast use a horse?	21. Name two events using a stick.
22. What is the shortest distance of a track running race?	23. Name two sports where an athlete jumps from a height.	24. Name three swimming events.

Road to the Olympic Games (cont.)

Directions: Cut apart the cards, match them to the questions on page 98, and then glue or tape them back-to-back.

1. marathon Move ahead 1 space.	2. 26 miles (26.2 miles) Move ahead 1 space.	3. summer Move ahead 1 space.
4. 5 Move ahead 1 space.	5. hockey Move ahead 2 spaces.	6. pole vault, skiing Move ahead 2 spaces.
7. swimming Move ahead 2 spaces.	8. downhill, slalom, giant slalom Move ahead 2 spaces.	9. poles, skis Move ahead 3 spaces.
10. 10 Move ahead 3 spaces.	11. men's/women's singles and pairs Move ahead 3 spaces.	12. cross-country skiing, shooting Move ahead 3 spaces.
13. figure skating and ice dancing Move ahead 4 spaces.	14. They lie on their backs. Move ahead 4 spaces.	15. open sled Move ahead 4 spaces.
16. discus, javlin, and shot put Move ahead 4 spaces.	17. floor exercises, vault Move ahead 5 spaces.	18. basketball or rhythmic gymnastics Move ahead 5 spaces.
19. gymnastics and diving Move ahead 5 spaces.	20. men's & women's vaulting & men's pommel horse routine Move ahead 5 spaces.	21. field hockey and ice hockey Move ahead 6 spaces.
22. 100 meters Move ahead 6 spaces.	23. diving, ski jumping Move ahead 6 spaces.	24. butterfly, backstroke, breaststroke, and freestyle Move ahead 6 spaces.

Road to the Olympic Games (cont.)

Directions: Cut apart the cards, match them to the answers on page 101, and then glue or tape them back-to-back.

1. Do most athletes win medals at the Olympic Games?	2. What was the prize for winner in the ancient Games?	3. Why did Jim Thorpe lose his medals?
4. What sport did Jim Abbott play?	5. What was the sport of Cassius Clay?	6. Who was Jesse Owens?
7. Before Johnny Weismuller played Tarzan, what was his sport?	8. What was Sonja Henie's sport?	9. What was Carl Lewis's sport?
10. What was the nickname of the great woman star of the 1932 Olympic Games?	11. Why did Ben Johnson lose his medal?	12. In what sport do they use a heavy stone and a broom?
13. What was the sport of Dick Button and Scott Hamilton?	14. What did Baron Pierre de Coubertin think more important than winning?	15. What was the sport of the 1992 U.S. "Dream Team"?
16. Who was James Connally?	17. How many Gold medals did Mark Spitz win in the 1972 Olympic Games?	18. Name a U.S. winner of the decathlon.
19. What sport did Olga Korbut popularize?	20. Name a U.S. diving Olympian whose daughter also won a medal in diving.	21. Who did Sammy Lee coach? In what sport?
22. In what sport did Anton Sailer and Jean Claude Killy star? Name the events each won.	23. Who was the West German skier who almost swept the Alpine events?	24. Name two figure skaters who turned professional and returned to compete in the 1992 Games.

Road to the Olympic Games (cont.)

Directions: Cut apart the cards, match them to the questions on page 100, and then glue or tape them back-to-back.

1. no Move ahead 2 spaces.	2. olive wreath Move ahead 2 spaces.	3. He had accepted money playing baseball. Move ahead 3 spaces.
4. baseball Move ahead 2 spaces.	5. boxing Move ahead 2 spaces.	6. U.S. track star, 1936 Olympic Games Move ahead 2 spaces.
7. swimming Move ahead 2 spaces.	8. figure skating Move ahead 2 spaces.	9. track and field Move ahead 3 spaces.
10. "Babe" Move ahead 3 spaces.	11. He tested positive for steroid use. Move ahead 3 spaces.	12. curling Move ahead 3 spaces.
13. figure skating Move ahead 4 spaces.	14. competing in the games Move ahead 4 spaces.	15. basketball Move ahead 4 spaces.
16. first American to win a gold medal Move ahead 4 spaces.	17. seven Move ahead 5 spaces.	18. Bob Mathias, Bill Toomey, Rafer Johnson, Bruce Jenner Move ahead 5 spaces.
19. gymnastics Move ahead 5 spaces.	20. Patricia McCormick Move ahead 5 spaces.	21. Greg Louganis, diving Move ahead 6 spaces.
22. Skiing, they both swept the Alpine events. Move ahead 6 spaces.	23. Rosi Mittermaier Move ahead 6 spaces.	24. Brian Boitano and Katerina Witt Move ahead 6 spaces.

Road to the Olympic Games (cont.)

Gameboard

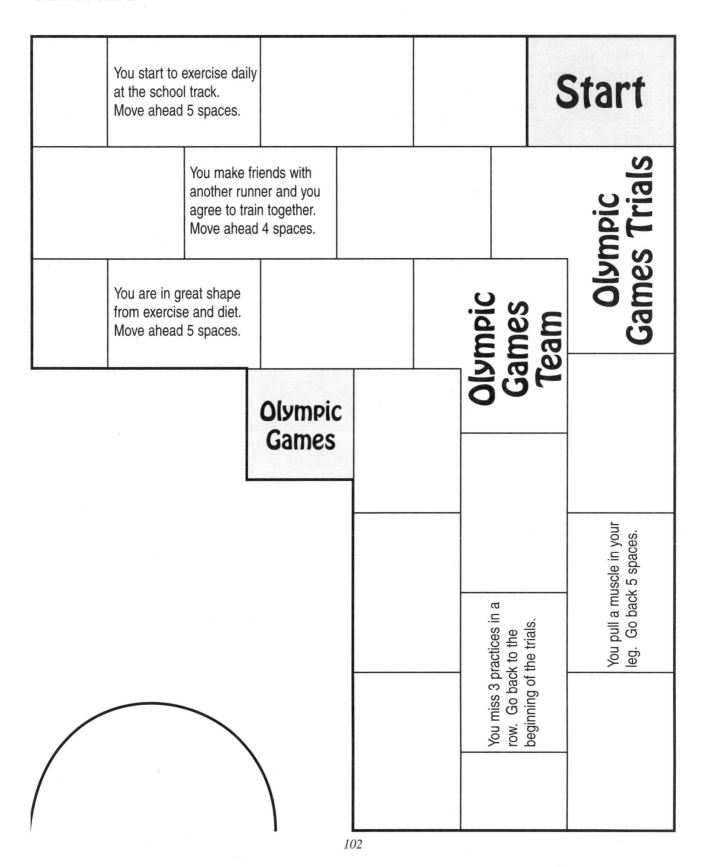

Road to the Olympic Games (cont.)

Gameboard

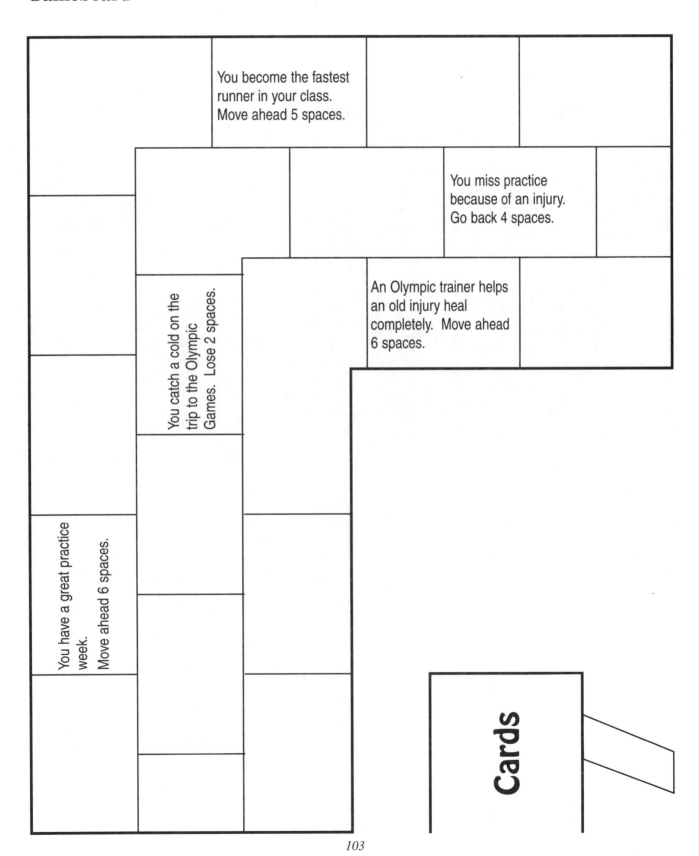

You become the fastest runner in your class. Move ahead 5 spaces.

You miss practice because of an injury. Go back 4 spaces.

An Olympic trainer helps an old injury heal completely. Move ahead 6 spaces.

You catch a cold on the trip to the Olympic Games. Lose 2 spaces.

You have a great practice week. Move ahead 6 spaces.

Cards

Road to the Olympic Games (cont.)

Gameboard

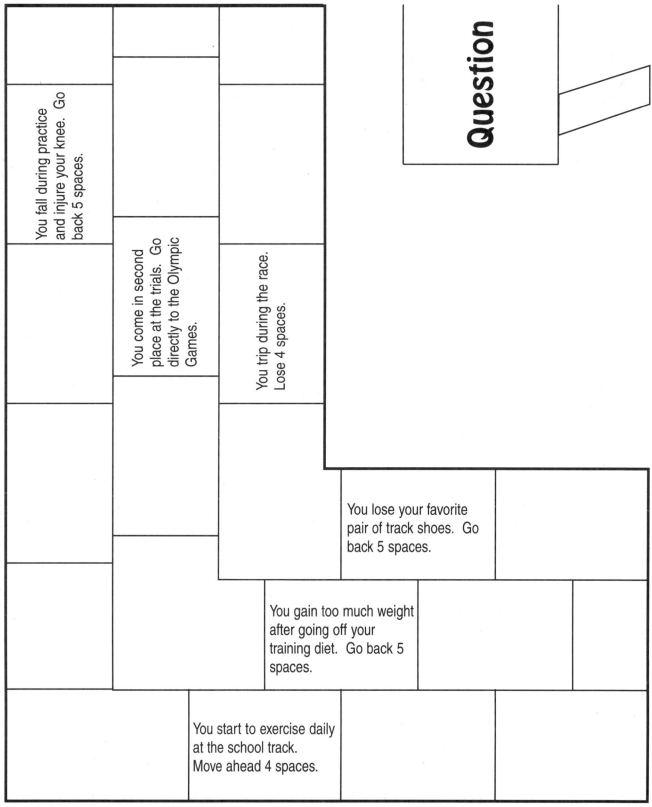

You fall during practice and injure your knee. Go back 5 spaces.

You come in second place at the trials. Go directly to the Olympic Games.

You trip during the race. Lose 4 spaces.

Question

You lose your favorite pair of track shoes. Go back 5 spaces.

You gain too much weight after going off your training diet. Go back 5 spaces.

You start to exercise daily at the school track. Move ahead 4 spaces.

Road to the Olympic Games (cont.)

Gameboard

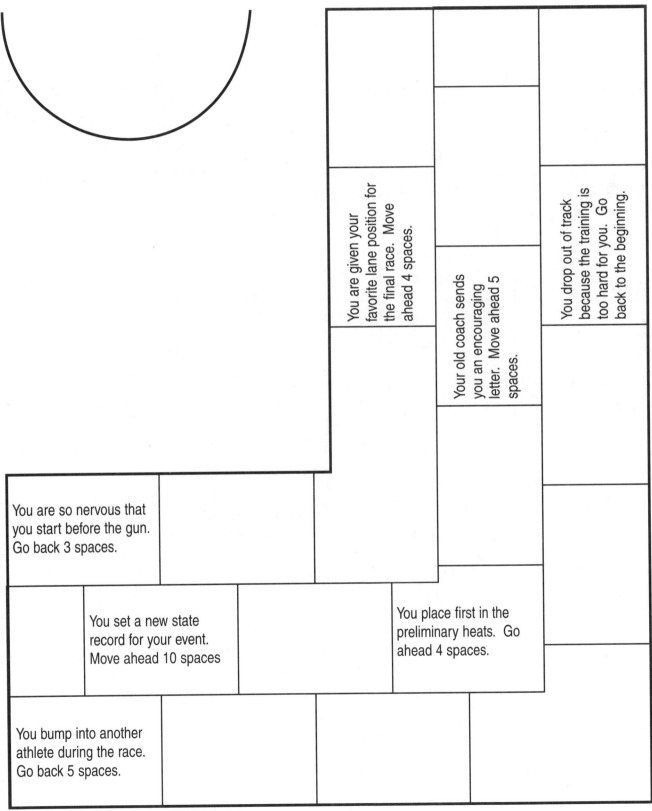

You are given your favorite lane position for the final race. Move ahead 4 spaces.

Your old coach sends you an encouraging letter. Move ahead 5 spaces.

You drop out of track because the training is too hard for you. Go back to the beginning.

You are so nervous that you start before the gun. Go back 3 spaces.

You set a new state record for your event. Move ahead 10 spaces

You place first in the preliminary heats. Go ahead 4 spaces.

You bump into another athlete during the race. Go back 5 spaces.

Academic Pentathlon

An academic pentathlon can be an excellent culmination for your Olympic Games unit. It gives all your students the opportunity to participate in a team event and perhaps come out as winners. (By now they should know that the greater reward is in participating.)

Getting Started

- Divide your class into teams of four to six students with a captain and manager for each team.

- Provide each team with a copy of the Olympic Games flag (page 123) and provide its manager with a box of crayons.

- Assign one of the colors of the Olympic Games rings to each of the five units in this book: Olympic Games History, Olympic Games Traditions, Olympic Games Sites, Olympic Games Events, and Olympic Games Competition. Each team in turn will be asked a question from one of the five units.

- For your convenience, it is suggested that you use the same questions as in the Road to the Olympic Games board game (pages 92–101). If your students have played the board game, they will have been exposed to all the questions. Choose beforehand those questions that best fit your class (either the easier or more challenging ones). Make one copy of each, cut them apart (no need to mount), and place them in five piles.

Objective

The object of the competition is to be the first team to complete the five rings of their Olympic flag. In order to do so, each team must answer correctly two questions from each unit presented in this book.

Academic Pentathlon (cont.)

The Competition

Each captain will choose a color for the team's turn and be asked a question from that unit. The team has ten seconds to confer before the captain gives an answer. If the answer is correct, the manager colors half a circle on the team's flag. An incorrect answer means the team forfeits its turn.

In the event of a tie, here are some suggested tie breakers. Each team can be given an allocated time to list:

— Sites of Olympic Games

— Gold medal winners

— Track stars

— Olympic Games summer sports
  (not individual events)

— Sites of Olympic Winter Games

— Skating stars

— Team Sports played in Olympic Games

— Olympic Games winter sports
  (not individual events)

Awards

All students competing should be given certificates of participation (page 120). Gold notary seals can be attached to the certificates of those on the first-place team and appropriately colored seals placed on the certificates of the second- and third-place finishers. If you are feeling particularly sweet, you could purchase some candy wrapped in gold, silver, and bronze (or brown) for the participants.

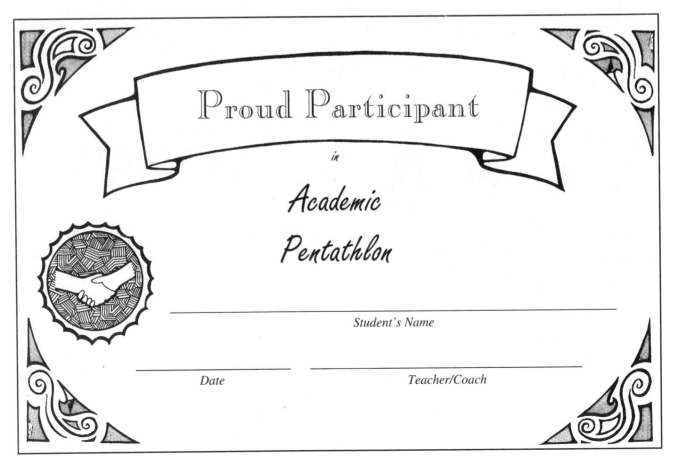

Proud Participant

in

Academic Pentathlon

_____
Student's Name

_____   _____
Date   *Teacher/Coach*

A Mini-Olympic Games

Once your class is familiar with the Olympic Games, stage your own mini-Olympic Games. The possibilities are endless, but here are some suggestions for staging one on a simple scale.

Planning the Games

As most schools have running lanes marked on the playground, choose four track and field events:

50- or 100-Meter Dash: Athletes run the length of a designated track.

Marathon: Athletes run a designated number of laps around the oval track, possibly a mile.

Discus Throw: Athletes throw a discus (use a softball or flying disc) for distance.

Long Jump: It is safer on most play areas to perform this from a standing position, rather than jumping from a running start.

Have your athletes sign up for the events in which they wish to participate. It is hoped all will sign up for at least one event. Nonparticipants in an event can help with timing or judging.

Scheduling the Games

Make a schedule for the events which is coordinated with your physical education program. Events with many participants may need preliminaries. There is a sample schedule below.

Prelims

Boys' Events

2. Boys' 50 m Dash — 9:20 a.m.
4. Boys' Marathon — 10:00 a.m.
6. Boys' Discus Throw — 10:40 a.m.
8. Boys' Long Jump — 11:20 a.m.

Girl's Events

1. Girls' 50 m Dash — 9:00 a.m.
3. Girls' Marathon — 9:40 a.m.
5. Girls' Discus Throw — 10:20 a.m.
7. Girls' Long Jump — 11:00 a.m.

Finals

Boys' 50 m Dash — 11:40 a.m.
Boys' Marathon — 12:00 p.m.
Boys' Discus Throw — 12:30 p.m.
Boys' Long Jump — 1:00 p.m.

Girls' 50 m Dash — 11:30 a.m.
Girls' Marathon — 11:50 a.m.
Girls' Discus Throw — 12:15 p.m.
Girls' Long Jump — 12:45 p.m.

A Mini-Olympic Games (cont.)

Running the Games

50- or 100-Meter Dash—To obtain the most accurate results, have each runner race the distance separately. Use a stopwatch to record the racer's time. The top qualifiers race in the finals. Visually judge the three medalists. An alternative plan is to line up the racers in each heat and have a helper start them off. Stand at the finish line and make a visual judgment of the first four runners. Do the same with each heat. Then have a run-off to determine the winners.

Marathon—Pair each of the athletes with a partner. (One of each pair runs while the partner counts his/her laps as completed.) Give the starting signal and start the stopwatch. When a runner has completed the designated number of laps, his/her partner calls out and checks the time on the stopwatch. A recorder keeps track of each runner's time. Repeat the procedure for the other partner.

Discus Throw—Each participant stands in place and hurls the softball forward. Judges in the field use chalk to mark its landing spot with the initials of the athlete.

Standing Long Jump—Before starting, use a meter stick to measure and chalk distances in meters on the area. Each athlete chooses a partner. The first participant stands with toes on the starting line. He/she jumps forward. The partner marks the spot of the athlete's body closest to the starting line. If he/she falls backward, the spot where the fingers touch is marked. If he/she falls forward, the spot where the heels touch is marked. Each athlete has three tries, and the best score is recorded.

109

A Mini-Olympic Games (cont.)

Awarding the Medals

Your awards ceremony can be simple. Students generally enjoy receiving their medals or certificates soon after the competition has been completed. Although students can create their own medals (page 121) for this competition, it is probably better to take some time to prepare medals they would enjoy keeping.

School supply stores offer ready-made medals, some self-adherent, in gold, silver, and bronze. These are particularly attractive and can be mounted on railroad board circles with a ribbon attached.

Certificates may be awarded (pages 118–119) in place of medals. Notary seals in appropriate colors may be attached for the three winners in each event. Be sure to award certificates to all participants in the mini-Olympic Games.

Going Farther

If you wish to have a more elaborate mini-Olympic Games, go for it. You can stage an Opening Ceremony with each athlete carrying a flag of a real or imaginary country. If your class is studying ancient Greece, your Opening Ceremony can reflect that of the ancient Games. (Athletes can wear sheet togas.)

If two or more classes participate in staging the mini-Olympic Games, your plans can be adjusted. Each class can represent a real or imaginary country. Additional events can be added, probably team games such as baseball, basketball, and volleyball.

For excellent ideas on conducting your own Olympic Games on a larger scale, be sure to check the publications of the U.S. Olympic Games Committee listed in the bibliography (pages 142–143), and books in the Official U.S. Olympic Games Committee Sport Series.

Your Own TV Coverage

When the Olympic Games are in town, the television cameras are everywhere. Reporters are stationed at the Olympic Village, at the airport, and at each venue or location where an event is scheduled. Your class will enjoy producing television coverage of the current or a past Olympic Games.

Begin by dividing your class and assigning parts to each student. The "cue cards" on the following pages can be used by each group of students to prepare their presentations.

The *anchor person* remains in the studio, giving the headlines of the day's Olympic Games and switching to reporters stationed about the "city."

A *weather person* should also be present in the studio. He/she can use maps to show the viewing audience what to expect in the way of weather the next day.

Field reporters will be stationed around the city.

- Those stationed in the Olympic Games Village can plan interviews with the athletes, both winners and losers.

- They will search for interesting stories about these young men and women and their families.

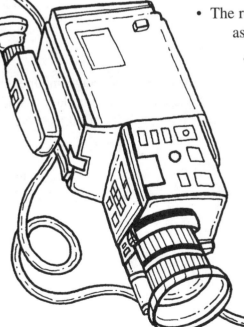

- The reporters at the airport will also do interviews as athletes come and go.

- Reporters at each venue will report on the sport at that venue. Their reports should include the rules and scoring of the events, as all the viewers may not be familiar with the sport. They may also be called on to give play-by-play accounts of events if the anchor person switches to their venue as an event is in progress.

Your Own TV Coverage (cont.)

The athletes' parts may be played by a "pool" of students who will take turns being various athletes when called upon by a reporter. And, of course, no telecast is complete without a "few words from our sponsors!" Have some students plan a few commercials.

Anchor Person

Your job is to be the host for your viewers. You will remain in the TV studio, open the program, and set the scene for the telecast. You may wish to write a script. However, you do not have to write down every word. Plan to "ad lib" or speak as you would to a friend.

Here are some script suggestions to get you started.

"Good evening, ladies and gentlemen. It is a pleasure to welcome you back to our coverage

of the (winter/summer) Games here in _____ . We will be

bringing you coverage today of the _____, _____ , and

_____ events as they occur.

Let's go live to our reporter _____ where

_____ is about to get underway.

Let's go live to the Olympic Games village where _____ is waiting

with the gold medal winner of the _____ event.

We pause now for the all-important weather report.

We will be right back after a few words from our sponsor."

Your Own TV Coverage (cont.)

Weather Person

Yours is quite an important job because athletes, coaches, and spectators depend on your information. To prepare your part, watch a weather report on TV. Take notes as you are watching. Using a map of your area, write out notes giving a weather report for the coming day. Practice giving the report in front of a mirror.

Reporters in the Field—At Olympic Games Village or the Airport

Choose the athlete you are going to interview. Prepare some interesting questions to ask. You can take one of your classmates from the "athlete pool." Tell him/her whose part he/she is taking and practice your interview together. Here are a few suggestions to help you get started.

- What are you doing to prepare for your event?
- How much practice do you get in each day?
- How is the weather here compared to your home?
- What memories will you carry back to your country?
- Are any of your family or friends with you here?
- After you compete, is there someone back home you will want to telephone?
- Now that your competition is complete, would you describe how it went?
- Are you happy with your performance?
- What are your plans about returning to compete four years from now?
- What do you do for fun here in the Olympic Games village?
- What do you want to see before you leave?
- How would you describe your Olympic Games experience?

Your Own TV Coverage (cont.)

Reporters in the Field—At Sports Venues

It is your job to share the excitement of the event you are covering with the television audience at home. Do some research on the rules and scoring of the event you are covering. Be ready to describe the live action for your viewers. Use the script below as a guide.

"Good evening, ladies and gentlemen, and welcome to _____, the site of the competition. This evening you will be seeing the finals of the _____. For those of you not familiar with this sport, let us take a few minutes to go over the rules. The scoring is as follows:

You also will be able to interview the athletes after they have competed. Have some questions ready.

Athletes—

You will be playing the part of athletes that the reporters choose to interview. The reporter should tell you ahead of time what athlete you are to "be." Try to find out something about him/her and be able to talk about your sport. You also have to be on your toes to answer personal questions about the athlete's family or other subjects with which you are unfamiliar. Use your imagination to make the interview exciting for your viewers on television.

Commercial Actors—

For this you probably do not need much coaching. You have undoubtedly watched thousands of hours of commercials in your lifetimes. Choose one which you think would be fun to produce. Assign parts to each member of your group. Write the parts. Decide whether you need props or costumes. Practice hard to make your sponsor proud.

Creating a Fine Arts Project

The early members of the Olympic Games Committee did not want the Olympic Games to be merely a sports spectacular. From 1912 through 1948, medals were also awarded for excellence in the fine arts. The rules stated that projects were to be entered in the fields of architecture, sculpture, painting, music, and literature. The works were to be inspired by sport.

Think about a project that you could do in one of the fields above. For literature, you may want to write a story about an athlete whose goal is the Olympic Games. If you like art, you may plan a painting depicting some phase of competition or use clay or another medium to sculpt an athlete in action. If you are musically inclined, you can come up with a song to cheer your team to victory. What ideas do you have? Use this form to plan your project.

Fine Arts Project

Name: _____

Fine Arts Field: _____

_____

_____

_____

Title of Project: _____

_____

_____

Description of Project: _____

_____

_____

_____

_____

_____

Additional Activities and Enrichment

This is not necessarily the end of your Olympic Games experience. Use your imagination and creativity to carry it into all areas of the curriculum. Here are a few suggestions.

If the Olympic Games are scheduled for a time when you are in school you can:

- Encourage your students to keep their own Olympic Games diaries. Write about what they most enjoyed watching each day.

- Have students choose a particular sport and keep a record of what is going on in each of the events.

- Record the times and scores of each day's events. Graph the results. Use the graphs to make up real-life word problems.

Make an attractive and useful display by expanding the time line (page 17) to fill one or more walls of your classroom. Mark each four-year span, beginning in 1896, and have your students draw pictures to represent the highlights of each Olympic Games. If you have the space, you can use an opposite wall to make a time line of the early Games. The wall in between can be numbered in centuries to show the great expanse of time between 776 B.C. and A.D. 2000+.

Vary this activity by having students write letters to their favorite athletes. The letters may then be traded with classmates who can answer them as that athlete.

Use the Olympic Games as a springboard into world geography. Your students can work in groups to list the countries more likely to host the Olympic Winter Games and the Olympic Games. They can become aware of the reverse seasons that caused Melbourne and Sydney to adjust the scheduling of the Olympic Games from the usual July/August start. They can recognize the effect of Mexico City's altitude on the athletes and the fact that fewer world records were expected to be broken there.

Take the opportunity to expand your students' mathematical understanding, using Olympic Games themes.

- Work with them to create additional activities with decimals (such as those on pages 63–64).

- Introduce or review the metric system of measurement. Plot 100 meters on the playground. Compare it to yards with which they may be more familiar.

Take a trip into the world of animals. Match the animal with the sport in which it could best excel (monkey—gymnastics, cheetah—100-meter dash). Have your students do science reports on these animal Olympians. (National Geographic Society has an excellent film on animal Olympians.)

Develop a mini-unit on health and nutrition. Discuss how an athlete in training needs the proper rest and diet. Include a study of the relationship of calories to various activities. Take off on your own and go for the gold.

Olympic Games Art Patterns

36 USC 220506

CONGRATULATIONS

You're a Winner!

Student's Name

Event

Place

School

Teacher/Coach

Date

Proud Participant

in the

Mini-Olympic

Games

Student's Name

Teacher/Coach

Date

Proud Participant

in the

Academic
Pentathlon

Student's Name

Date

Teacher/Coach

Design an Olympic Games Medal

Directions: Cut out the three patterns and create designs for gold, silver, and bronze medals. Then cut out cardboard pieces that are the same size as the pattern pieces. Glue each side to a piece of the cardboard and then glue the two pieces together. Color them and add a ribbon to make them complete.

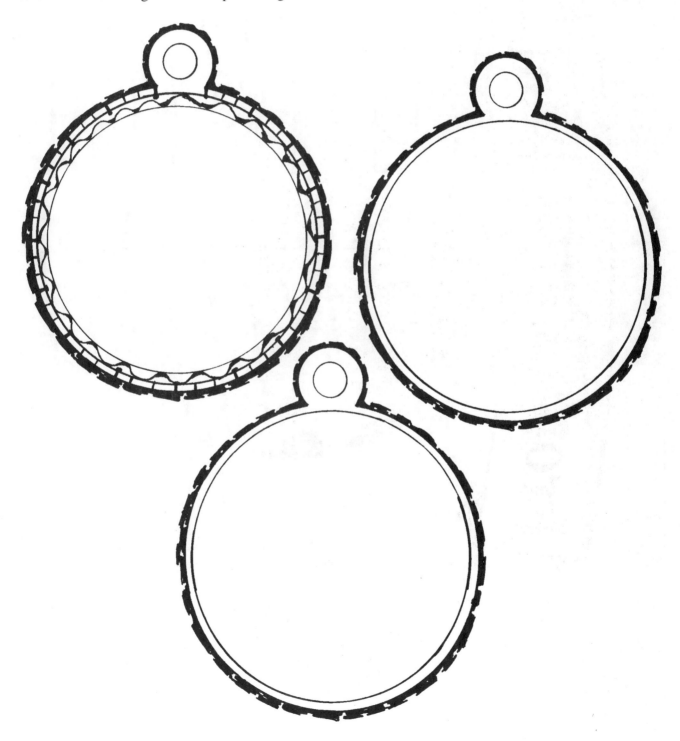

U.S. Flag

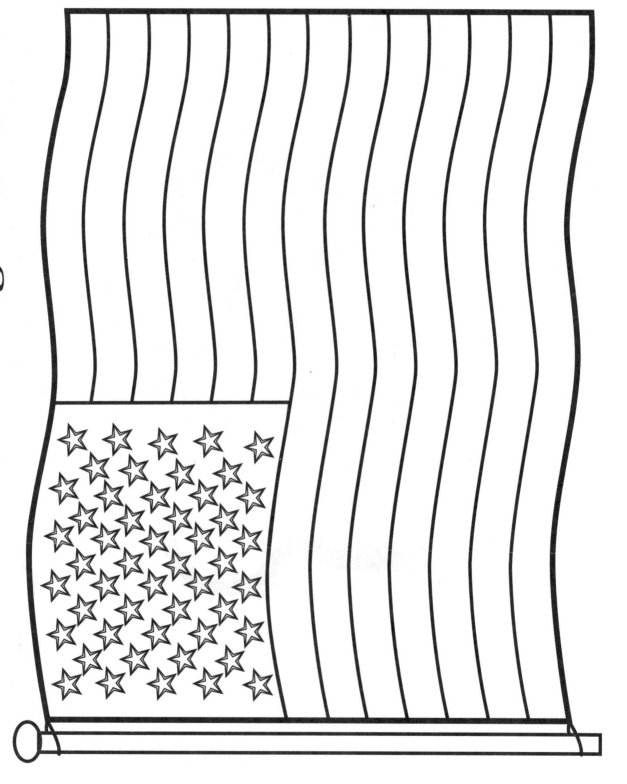

Olympic Games Ring

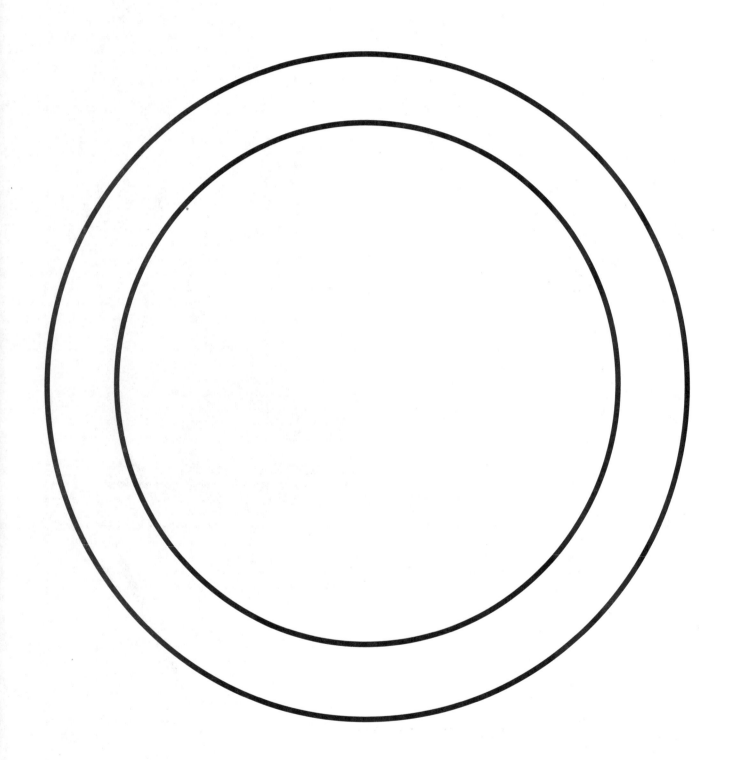

Olympic Games Torch

World Map

World Map (cont.)

Winter Events Logos

BIATHLON

BOBSLED

CURLING

FIGURE SKATING

ICE HOCKEY

LUGE

Winter Events Logos (cont.)

SKIING

SNOWBOARDING

Summer Events Logos

SPEED SKATING

ARCHERY

ATHLETICS

Summer Events Logos

BADMINTON

BASEBALL

BASKETBALL

BOXING

CANOE/KAYAK

CYCLING

Summer Events Logos (cont.)

DIVING

EQUESTRIAN

FENCING

FIELD HOCKEY

GYMNASTICS

JUDO

Summer Events Logos (cont.)

MODERN PENTATHLON

ROWING

SHOOTING

SOCCER

SOFTBALL

SWIMMING

Summer Events Logos (cont.)

SYNCHRONIZED SWIMMING

TABLE TENNIS

TAEKWONDO

TEAM HANDBALL

TENNIS

TRIATHLON

Summer Events Logos (cont.)

VOLLEYBALL

WATER POLO

WEIGHT LIFTING

WRESTLING

YACHTING

Olympic Games T-shirt

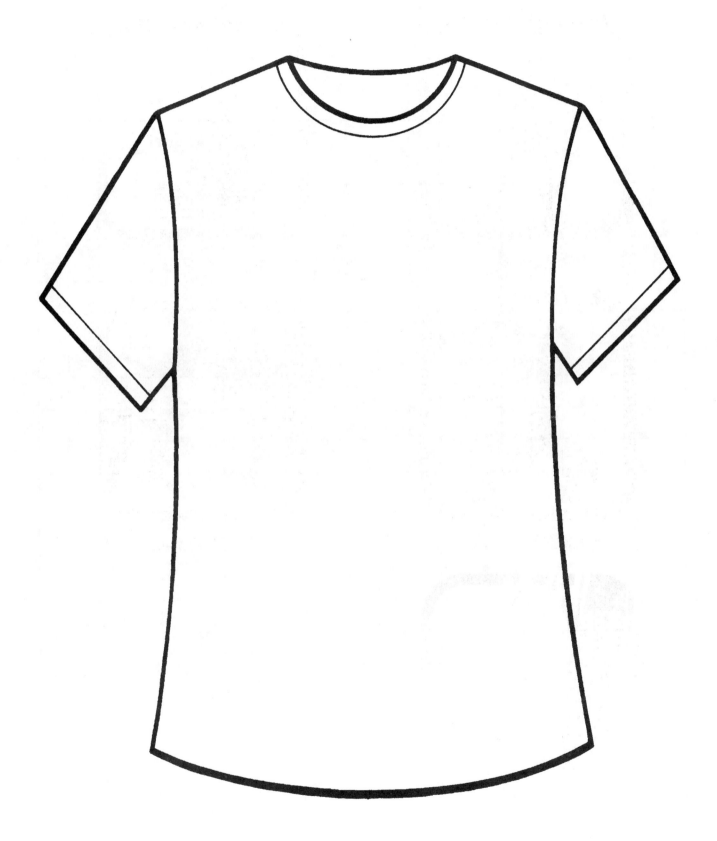

Graph Paper

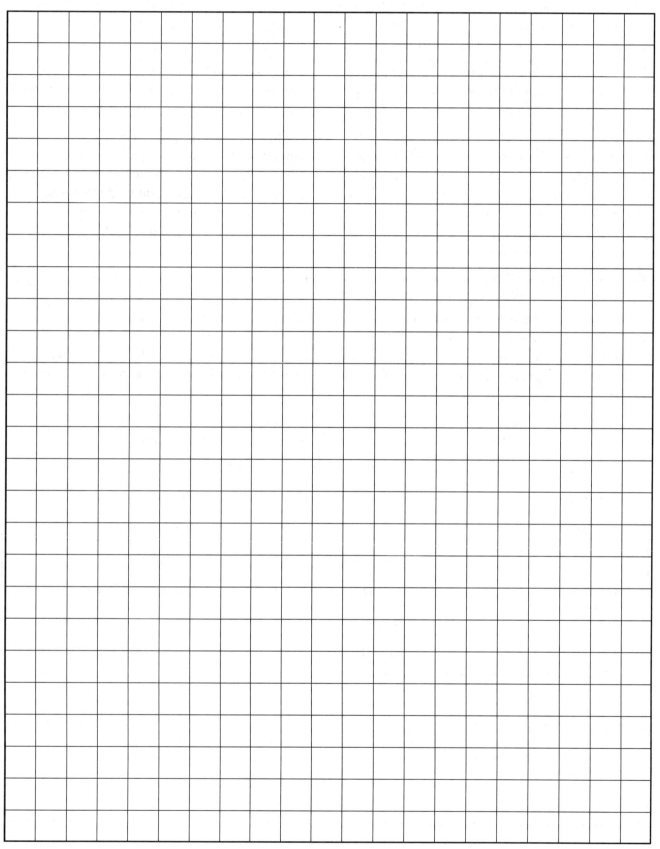

The Paralympic Games

The first Paralympic Games were held in Rome in 1960 for four hundred athletes, representing 23 countries. They are held every four years following the Olympic Games. The vision for the events came from Dr. Ludwig Guttman of the Stoke-Mandeville Hospital in England. He worked with many veterans of World War II who suffered from spinal cord injuries. He dreamed of a world class event to spotlight athletes with physical disabilities.

The Paralympics are not to be confused with the Special Olympics, a participatory event where all contenders receive medals. The Paralympics is a competition of elite, world class, well trained disabled athletes. The term paralympics actually means "next to" or "parallel" to the regular Olympic Games.

In 1988, The Paralympic Games were held immediately following the Olympic Games in Seoul, Korea, using the same Olympic facilities. In September 1992, again following the Olympic Games, Barcelona welcomed 3,044 athletes to the IX Paralympiad. From opening and closing ceremonies to competitions in Olympic venues, the 1992 Paralympic Games mirrored the Olympic celebration held three weeks earlier. More than 4,000 athletes are expected at the Sydney 2000 Paralympic Games. They will be competing in 18 different sports, many of which are also on the Olympic program. Sailing and Wheelchair Rugby are the new sports for Sydney.

Paralympic competitors include athletes who are blind or visually impaired, paraplegics (whose legs are partially or totally paralyzed), quadriplegics (whose arms and legs are partially or totally paralyzed), people with cerebral palsy, amputees (who have a limb partially or completely removed), dwarfs, and those with other disabilities. The athletes are selected to represent their countries based on performances at qualifying events. Minor modifications are sometimes made to the rules of each sport to accommodate some of the athletes' disabilities. Athletes are classified according to the severity of disability and compete against athletes with similar disabilities.

The Paralympic Summer Sports Program

Archery	Football (soccer)	Swimming
Athletics	Goalball	Table Tennis
Basketball	Judo	Tennis
Boccia	Lawn Bowls	Volleyball
Cycling	Powerlifting	Wheelchair Rugby
Equestrian	Sailing	
Fencing	Shooting	

The Paralympic Winter Sports Program

Biathlon	Speed Skating	Cross-Country Skiing
Ice Hockey	Alpine Skiing	

Answer Key

Page 14

1. Olympia
2. citizens
3. athletes
4. foot
5. gods
6. five
7. chariot
8. horse
9. pentathlon
10. wrestling
11. rod
12. running
13. hoplite
14. excluded

Milo of Croton

Ox

Page 17

Among acceptable answers:

1896—First Modern Olympic Games

1900—women (and horses) included in events

1912—electrical timers introduced

1916—WWI canceled Games

1924—First Winter Games

1932—electronic judging, first Olympic Games Village

1936—radio broadcast Games, torch carried

1940–1944—WWII canceled Games

1960—TV coverage of the Games

1968—Drug testing began

1980—Many countries boycotted Games

1984—China competed for the first time in 30 years

1994—Winter Games scheduled in separate year

1996—Centennial Games celebrated in Atlanta

Page 35
Olympic Winter Games

1. Austria 1964
2. Canada 1988
3. France 1924, 1968
4. Germany 1936
5. Italy 1956
6. Japan 1972, 1998
7. Norway 1952
8. USA 1932, 1960
9. Yugoslavia 1980
10. Switzerland 1928, 1948
11. Blank
12. Blank

Page 36–37
Olympic Games

1. Australia 1956, 2000
2. Belgium 1920
3. Canada 1976
4. Sweden 1912
5. Finland 1952
6. France 1900, 1924
7. Germany 1936
8. Greece 1896 (2004)
9. Italy 1960
10. Mexico 1968
11. Netherlands 1928
12. Spain 1992
13. Korea (South) 1988
14. Great Britain (England) 1908
15. USA 1904, 1932, 1984, 1996
16. Japan 1964
17. Russia 1980
18. Blank

Answer Key (cont.)

Page 39

1. Paris, France 2. Los Angeles 1932 3. Athens 1896 4. Los Angeles 1984 5. St. Moritz 1948

Page 51

Ball: baseball, basketball, field hockey, rhythmic gymnastics, shot put, soccer, softball, table tennis, team handball, tennis, volleyball, water polo

Net: badminton, basketball, field hockey, soccer, table tennis, tennis, volleyball, water polo

Water: canoeing, diving, kayaking, modern pentathlon, rowing, swimming, synchronized swimming, water polo, yachting

Horse: equestrian, modern pentathlon

No special equipment: gymnastics-floor, running, judo, long jump, swimming, taekwondo, wrestling

Page 52

Throwing: baseball, basketball, discus, hammer throw, javelin, rhythmic gymnastics, shot put, soccer, softball, team handball, water polo

Athletics (Track and Field): decathlon, discus, hammer throw, high jump, hurdles, javelin, running, long jump, pole vault, marathon, relays, shot put, triple jump

Long distances: cycling, equestrian 3-day, marathon, pentathlon, triathlon, yachting

Kicking: judo, soccer, taekwondo

Team Events: baseball, basketball, field hockey, soccer, softball, team handball, volleyball, water polo

Pages 56–57

Events using skis—alpine, biathlon, cross-country, freestyle, Nordic, and ski jumping

Events taking place on the ice—bobsledding, curling, figure skating, ice dancing, ice hockey, luge, short track skating, and speed skating

Events done in pairs—bobsledding, figure skating, luge, and ice dancing

Team events—bobsledding, figure skating, ice dancing, ice hockey, and luge

Events needing special equipment—Alpine skiing, biathlon, bobsledding, cross-country skiing, figure skating, curling, freestyle skiing, ice dancing, ice hockey, luge, Nordic combined skiing, ski jumping, short track skating, and speed skating

Events where women compete—Alpine skiing, biathlon, bobsledding, cross-country skiing, figure skating, freestyle skiing, ice dancing, luge, ski jumping, short track skating, snowboarding, and speed skating

Events using skates—figure skating, ice dancing, ice hockey, short track skating, and speed skating

Events covering long distances—biathlon, cross-country skiing, and Nordic-combined skiing

Individual events—Alpine skiing, biathlon, cross-country skiing, figure skating, freestyle skiing, luge, Nordic combined skiing, short track skiing, ski jumping, snowboarding, and speed skating

Events with jumping—freestyle skiing and ski jumping

Page 53

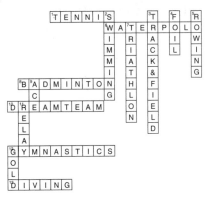

Page 58

139

Answer Key (cont.)

Page 61

1. puck
2. five
3. oar
4. paddle
5. glove
6. hurdle
7. run
8. rink
9. ten
10. round
11. stick
12. hoop
13. lie
14. blade
15. throw
16. marathon
17. court
18. pin
19. equestrian
20. Nordic
21. foot
22. sled
23. decathlon
24. sailboat
25. platform

Page 62

1. decathlon
2. ancient pentathlon
3. biathlon
4. modern pentathlon
5. heptathlon
6. triathlon
7. answers will vary

Pages 64

Freestyle		Breaststroke	
51.89		1:04.38	
51.79	.10	1:04.37	.01
51.70	.09	1:04.26	.11
51.68	.02	1:04.23	.03
50.81	.87	1:03.43	.80
49.99	.82	1:03.11	.32
	1.90		1.27

Backstroke		Butterfly	
57.69		55.81	
57.49	.20	55.11	.70
57.28	.21	55.09	.02
57.22	.06	54.65	.44
56.34	.88	54.50	.15
55.49	.85	54.35	.15
	2.20		1.46

Slalom		Giant Slalom	
1:33.24		1:30.49	
1:32.31	.93	1:30.44	.05
1:32.24	.07	1:30.40	.04
1:32.20	.04	1:29.95	.45
1:30.87	1.33	1:29.25	.70
1:30.54	.33	1:29.13	.12
	2.70		1.36

Downhill	
1:48.58	
1:48.48	.10
1:47.71	.77
1:47.50	.21
1:46.68	.82
1:46.16	.52
	2.42

Challenge: .01 in the breaststroke

Fourth place was only .02 in freestyle

Answer Key (cont.)

Page 75

Immediate Effects

Good: aggressiveness leading to harder training, some muscle buildup

Bad: "roid" rage, baldness, for women—deepening of voice and whiskers

Long-term Effects

Good: none

Bad: liver problems, cancer, reproductive system affected, bone growth slowed

Page 77

Page 78

Left-handed, Abbott, Michigan, Big Ten, victory, Japan

Wilma, walk, basketball, track, bronze, three

Ewry, wheelchair, leg, Paris, Saint Louis, London,

Fanny, World War, thirty, track, field, Takacs, pistol, right, shoot, podium, gold

Page 82

1	2	3	4	5	6	7	8	9	10	11	12	13	14	15	16	17
T	H	I	S	S	U	R	E	I	S	T	H	E	P	I	T	S	!

Bibliography

Anderson, Dave. *The Story of Basketball.* Morrow, 1988.

Arnold, Caroline. *The Summer Olympic Games.* Franklin Watts, 1991.
    Olympic Winter Games. Franklin Watts, 1991.

Bailey, Donna. *Cycling.* Raintree, 1990.

Baker, William J. *Jesse Owens: An American Life.* The Free Press, 1988.

Barry, James P. *The Berlin Olympics, 1936: Black American Athletics Counter Nazi Propaganda.* Franklin Watts, 1975.

Benagh, Jim. *Incredible Olympic Feats.* McGraw-Hill, 1976.

Birenbaum, Barbara. *The Olympic Glow.* Peartree, 1994.

Bloom, Marc. *Basketball.* Scholastic, 1991.

Broklin, Yuri. *The Big Red Machine: The Rise and Fall of Soviet Olympic Champions.* Random House, 1978.

Carlson, Lewis H. and John J. Fogarty. *Tales of Gold.* Contemporary Books, 1987.

Carrier, Roch. *The Boxing Champion.* Tundra Books, 1991.

Chester, David. *The Olympic Games Handbook: An Authentic History of Both the Ancient and Modern Olympic Games, Complete Results and Records.* Scribner, 1975.

Christesen, Barbara. *First Olympic Games.* Contemporary Perspectives, 1978.

Cohen, Daniel. *Wrestling Superstars.* Pocket, 1985.

Coote, James. *A Picture History of the Olympics.* Macmillan, 1972.

Dershem, Kurt. *The Olympians.* Iron Crown, 1990.

Devaney, John. *Great Olympic Champions.* Putnam, 1967.

Dieterich, Michelle. *Skiing.* Lerner Publications, 1992.

Dress, Ludwig. *Olympia: Gods, Artists, and Athletes.* Praeger, 1968.

Duden, Jane. *Olympics.* Macmillan Child Group., 1991.

Duder, Tessa. *Journey to Olympia.* Scholastic, 1992.

Durant, John. *Highlights of the Olympics: From Ancient Times to the Present.* Hastings House, 1977.

Evan, Jeremy. *Skiing.* Macmillan Child Group., 1992.

Finlay, Moses I. and H. W. Pleket. *The Olympic Games: The First Thousand Years.* Viking Press, 1976.

Finlayson, Ann. *Stars of the Modern Olympics.* Garrard, 1967.

Bibliography (cont.)

Fisher, Leonard. *Olympians: Greek Gods & Goddesses of Ancient Greece.* Holiday, 1989.

Fraden, Dennis B. *Olympics.* Children's Press, 1983.

Gault, Frank and Clare. *Stories from the Olympics: From 776 B.C. to Now.* Walker and Co., 1976.

Gelman, Steve. *Young Olympic Champions.* Grossett and Dunlap, 1973.

Girardi, Wolfgang. *Olympic Games.* Franklin Watts, 1972.

Glubok, Shirley and Alfred Tamarin. *Olympic Games in Ancient Greece.* HarperCollins Children's Books, 1976.

Greenberg, Stan. *The Guiness Book of Olympics Facts and Feats.* Guiness Superlatives Limited, 1983.

Gutman, Bill. *Basketball.* Marshall Cavendish, 1990.
    Swimming. Marshall Cavendish, 1990.
    Track & Field. Marshall Cavendish, 1990.
    Volleyball. Marshall Cavendish, 1990.

Hall, Jackie. *Skiing & Snow Sports.* Franklin Watts, 1990.

Harvey, Frommer. *Olympic Controversies.* Franklin Watts, 1987.

Jarrett, William S. *Timetable of Sports History: The Olympic Games.* Facts on File, 1990.

Knight, Theodore. *Olympic Games.* Lucent Books, 1991.

Laklan, Carli. *Golden Girls: True Stories of Olympic Women Stars.* McGraw-Hill, 1980.

Los Angeles Times. *The Los Angeles Times Book of the 1984 Olympic Games.* Harry N. Abrams, Inc., 1984.

McDonald, Kendall. *Divers.* Garrett Ed. Corp., 1992.

Pearson, David. *Gymnastics.* Sterling, 1991.

Pizer, Vernon. *Glorious Triumphs: Athletes Who Conquered Adversity.* Dodd, Mead and Co., 1980.

Sandelson, Robert. *Swimming & Diving.* Macmillan Child Group, 1991.

Schaap, Dick. *The Olympics.* Alfred A. Knopf, 1975.
    1984 Olympic Games. Random House, 1984.

Schoor, Gene. *The Jim Thorpe Story.* Julian Messner, 1951.

Segrave, Jeffrey O. and Donald Chu, Editors. *Olympic Games in Transition.* Human Kinetics Books, 1988.

Tatlow, Peter. *The Olympics.* Bookwright Press, 1988.

Walsh, John. *The Summer Olympics.* Franklin Watts, 1979.

Ward, Carl. *Hockey.* Sterling, 1991.